HOLDING THE HAND OF A KING

FORMING A DEEPER RELATIONSHIP WITH GOD THE FATHER

BY

KATHRYN J. BAIN

FOREWORD

BY

GERMAINE COPELAND

INSPIRATIONAL SPEAKER AND BEST-SELLING AUTHOR OF
THE PRAYERS THAT AVAIL MUCH FAMILY SERIES
FOUNDER OF WORD MINISTRIES (WMI) HTTPS://PRAYERS.ORG/

Book cover design by Jessi Bain and Two Stone Lions Press
All rights reserved.
Interior design by Bob Sharpe – Two Stone Lions Press

Published in the United States of America
by Two Stone Lions Press

ISBN-10: 1-62390-067-0
ISBN-13: 978-1-62390-067-0

Religion - Spirituality

HOLDING THE HAND OF A KING

BY

KATHRYN J. BAIN

FOREWORD

BY

GERMAINE COPELAND

FOUNDER OF WORD MINISTRIES (WMI) HTTPS://PRAYERS.ORG/

FOREWORD

Far too many adult children find themselves with unresolved anger and negative feelings they try to keep buried. However as someone has said, "Feelings buried alive never die." This book is the account of a woman who was abandoned by her father, a social outcast at school and who turned to alcohol to fill the hole in her soul.

Kathryn J. Bain has written an open, personal account of the inner journey of her struggle with alcohol, self-rejection, and her sense of unworthiness. It is my prayer that her story will give you hope and that you will experience transformation as you discover the God who loves you unconditionally. Her view of God was formed out of her childhood hurts, disappointments and her need for a dad who loved her.

My story is different, but I struggled with the same issues and relate to her fears, self-hatred and lack of trust. Before my encounter with the God of the Bible, I did not like Him, and I believed that He did not like me because I could never measure up. I considered Him harsh and punitive. There were times I felt as though I would fly into a million fragments and I wanted to be whole.

Do you want to be whole? Allow Kathryn to introduce you to a God who is a Father that will never leave you, or forsake you, or leave you without support.

If you want nothing to do with God as I did at one time, Kathryn's story will introduce you to the God who is real, the God of the Bible.

If you struggle with hurts from your childhood, painful words that devalued you as a person, or a birth mother or father who could not nurture or care for you, Kathryn's book is for you. She will teach you how to overcome your fear of trusting the God who loves you unconditionally. His love is not based on anything you have done or haven't done; His love is who He is.

Over the years I've met many women who declared they would never refer to God as Father. One young woman who was working on her Ph.D. asked how she could ever learn to trust a God she could not see, when she had taken care of her parents since she was five years old. Her dad did not nurture her, but looked to her to take care of him and her mother. Yet, over time, she chose to believe the God of the Bible.

God is the same yesterday, today, and forever. You can always depend on Him. The transformation in you happens as you learn who the Creator of the universe is. He knew you before you were born and His thoughts toward you are for good and not evil.

Here in the pages of this narrative, you will find practical steps that will help you. I pray that all may go well with you and that you may be in good health (mentally, emotionally and physically) as it goes will with your soul. (3 John 2) You can be made whole and know the Father-God who loves you unconditionally!

~ Germaine Copeland
Inspirational speaker and best-selling author of the
Prayers That Avail Much family series, and other publications.
Founder of Word Ministries (WMI)
https://prayers.org/

This change begins when you "Verbally confess that Jesus is Lord and fully trust in your inner self that God brought him back to life, and you will be made whole." (Romans 10:10)

CONTENTS

Introduction

The strength of a woman is not measured
by the impact that all her hardships in life
have had on her; but the strength of a woman
is measured by the extent of her refusal
to allow those hardships to dictate her
and who she becomes.
—*C. Joybell C.,*
Author, Leading Thought Influencer[i]

My hair is too thin, I have crepey skin, there's a dry patch on my wrist, my middle fingernails split (put that into it what you want), don't even talk gravity to me, there are stretch marks from giving birth to two kids, cellulite, my thighs seem to have some sort of magnetic pull toward each other (no gap there). My knees are fat, and there's even a toenail fungus thing going on every once in a while.

And that's just the outside. Mentally I can't recall anyone's name, and I'm judgmental. Physically, there's sciatica, and the list goes on and on.

From my head to my feet, I can find plenty I don't like about myself. And I'll bet you're a lot like me. Maybe not the toenail issue, but I'll guarantee your list is just as long.

Funny how easy it is for us to come up with flaws. Not so easy to come up with things we like. It doesn't help that every model and television starlet makes us feel inferior. I know deep inside those models are just cartoon caricatures of the real person, and movie stars wear an inch of makeup and hire personal trainers to keep them in shape. But, no matter how many times I tell myself they aren't that beautiful, my self-esteem still suffers on those days I need to lie down on the bed to get my jeans zipped.

It doesn't help that some husbands won't take his eyes off that beautiful woman on TV, yet they barely gave a grunt hello when they walked through the door that evening.

We tend to forget that what Hollywood shows us is not real. The magazine covers are lies. It's what God tells us that is important. And He says we are His daughters. He loves us no matter what we look like, how we feel about ourselves, or what anyone else has said about us.

And our looks aren't the only issues that drive us to the edge. How about our behavior?

As Christian women, we're told to be kind and forgiving. Yet, at times, my actions and words tear others down instead of building them up like they're supposed to.

I end the day flopping into bed, hoping I'll behave better tomorrow. I forget about the good things and only focus on how I messed up. And then I get emotional. I allow my feelings to ignore God's whispers of how well I did do, and how much He loves me.

Can any of you relate?

At least I'm single so there's no husband snoring beside me or off playing golf while I'm having my pity-party.

Most women know if you tell your husband you want to talk about your feelings, he can't get out of the house fast enough.

Men hate to talk about feelings, yet women have an abundance. Some days emotions feel like a four-letter word. How many times have you gotten mad at your husband for leaving his wet towel on the bathroom floor? Yet, within minutes a commercial on life insurance has you crying, praying nothing bad happens to the slob.

Strong emotions are part of a woman's life. Unfortunately, they can go on and off like a light. I don't know about you, but some days I can't seem to control the switch. God made us to be caring and compassionate creatures. As females, most of us are understanding, gracious, and loving, but if someone were to attack our child, the momma bear comes out.

There hasn't been a time when you haven't been passionate one moment and angry the next. Love and tenderness combine with self-pity and doubt creating a combination that we don't even understand. How can we expect a man to get it when one moment we're Jekyll, the next Hyde?

I can't help but wonder if some of my insecurities were developed because of my alcoholic father. He was never around much, and when he was, most of those times weren't pleasant.

Growing up, I never felt like I was worth much. I wasn't pretty, at least not by society's standards.

It didn't help that my sister was thin and had naturally curly blond hair. I was overweight and had straight thin hair, the color of dishwater blonde – whatever that meant. I looked like a ragamuffin most of the time. For Christmas, we both got the same style clothing, which if any of you know anything about fashion, what looks good on someone thin, doesn't look good on someone overweight. I always thought of myself as ugly.

My understanding is I'm not alone. A lot of other women fall into this category of abandonment because of our father issues. A good deal of our self-hate comes from a lack of love as a child, whether real or perceived to be real.

For years, I doubted God's love for me. I saw Him through the eyes of a girl who felt abandoned psychologically. I'm sure some of you lived the same story - a childhood involving a father who abandoned you physically, emotionally, or both. And let's not forget those who were abusive.

That's who this book is for. Women with self-hate and flaws they feel need to be repaired in order to be happy. Those who lacked a strong father-daughter bond and now have feelings of inadequacy. Those women, like me, who had a father who never knew how to show love.

Women who want a close relationship with God, but see Him as some out of reach deity.

Unfortunately, society has virtually tossed fathers aside without any thought as to how important they are in their children's lives. Studies have been done over the years detailing the importance of fathers in their son's lives. It's just becoming clear how much a girl needs her father as well. Without a loving father, a girl will grow into an insecure woman. Her relationship with men suffers and her faith suffers as well.

Too many children grow up without a father these days which makes it hard to relate to a divine being that calls himself Father. And the devil keeps reminding us that if our own father didn't love us, how can God?

If your earthly father rejected you, chances are you still feel that rejection today. Who wants to worship a God who might disappear in the same way?

And yes, even Christian women can feel the rejections of their past keeping them from having a deep relationship with God. They allow themselves to be held in bondage by their feelings of inadequacies every day. By allowing our emotions to take lead over our lives, we become easy prey for the devil. He likes to chip away at our faith a little a time. He'll play on our emotions to make us think we are not worthy of God's love. Yet, there is nothing further from the truth.

We must see God as our Father even at times when it's not easy. Emotional issues creep up on us daily, even hourly, but, God is more than just a creator, more than just some long-bearded aberration in the sky. He is, and always has been, the one constant in our lives that we can count on.

Now, you might be asking yourself just who do I think I am, writing a book about God's love? I'm no minister. I have no Ph.D. after my name. I'm just a paralegal by day and a small-time Christian author by night.

My only experience is I've been where you are. You see, I know those feelings of not being good enough.

It took me years to realize I was not truly happy and without

God's deep love, I could never know His joy.

I think one of the saddest things I see is when a Christian woman believes she is not worthy to be the Lord's daughter. She might feel abandoned, maybe unable to hear God's voice. She might even think any sin has caused her to go too far for God to ever forgive.

Isn't that why dad left? Because I did…?

I hope the message of this book brings you joy and comfort in knowing you ARE a king's daughter. Not just any king, but the King of Kings.

There are Bible verses, quotes, and prayers along the way to help you with your journey to princessdom. Just a smorgasbord of peace and joy in the hope that something will help bring you into a deeper relationship with God. Please feel free to copy them and tape them to your mirror, refrigerator, computer screen, or wherever they will be most effective. There are also extra Bible verses and questions at the end of each section to help you dig a bit deeper into this journey of becoming God's true daughter. I've also added a prayer at the end of each chapter to use or you can make up one of your own.

And be aware, I'm a list person, so you'll find plenty in this book.

Only by facing the truth about how you view yourself and your past can you have a future filled with complete joy. We are all God's daughters, and He is our Father. That is a truth that can set you onto a life of joy and happiness if you're willing to accept it.

It's time to stop lying to that woman in the mirror. Listen to the words of your Father instead. He likes to brag on His most prized possession – you. God can't wait to announce that each one of us is His child. And a father likes nothing more than to hold onto his daughter when she needs Him most.

There is no greater love than our Father's love. His love is bigger than any earthly fathers. So, hold your head up straight, grab hold of that tiara, and let's step into a deeper understand of God the King, God the Father.

The Christian life is not about
all the things we do for God–
it's about being loved by Him,
loving Him in return
and walking in intimate union
and communion with Him.
—Nancy Leigh DeMoss,
Christian Radio Host[iii]

Prayer to Get Us Started

Stop now and pray before you go on to the first chapter. Below is a prayer I've written. Feel free to use it or say one of your own.

Dear Lord,
I pray you help me discover a deeper relationship with the real you, God the Father. I pray I can put aside my past hurts in order to draw into a deeper relationship with You. Please hold me when I need it, at those times I feel the most alone and betrayed when I recall the lack of love from my natural father. Let me know and feel that I am loved. Let me be aware of Your presence when I need You most, and that no matter how I was treated by my father, remind me You were always there with me, and You never abandoned me.
In Jesus name,
Amen

CHAPTER ONE
Let Me Introduce You
to Your Father's Love

For God so loved the world,
that he gave his only Son,
that whoever believes in him
should not perish but have eternal life.
—*John 3:16*

If someone were to ask you to state in one word what the story of the Bible is about, what would you say? Jesus? Faith? Forgiveness?

True, but I'd say it's more a story of love. The love of a Father for his children.

Before we go further, let's define exactly what a father is. Most of us define the noun use of father as a provider or paternal protector. However, you might be surprised to find that dictionary.com defines the verb use of father as "author of" and to "assume as his own."

I love the notion that God assumes us as His own. Basically, we are His.

Now, let me ask you, what does a father do? Come up with some words to describe a father's job. I'll bet some of the words used were things like comforter, protector, or provider.

How about abuser or neglecter?

Depends on who you ask. To some, these two words might describe how their opinion of a father. Unfortunately, they might also picture God the Father the same way.

I did for a long time.

My earthly father was an alcoholic. He was abusive, verbally, emotionally, and sometimes physically. I saw things in the negative for a long time, including God. As far as I was concerned, God was a mean, judgmental being in the sky I couldn't rely on. He was just a spiritual being who was far off and untouchable. He had too many rules I could never live up to and didn't want to. He was certainly not a deity I could have a relationship with.

A father's job is to provide shelter and food for his children. He is to love the mother and make sure everything runs smoothly in the family. Unfortunately, too many fathers these days are abusive, or they walk away because it's easier than being the head of the family.

I don't know about you,
but if the foundation
of God's love was my actions,
I'd be in a lot of trouble.

Women who grew up in these types of families tend to not trust God. They see Him through the eyes of a child who was abandoned, either emotionally or physically. We don't think of him as a provider, but as a God who's out there waiting for us to screw up. So we turn away from him the way our earthly fathers turned away from us. Or we never get the close relationship we yearn for.

How can I be close to God the Father when John the father was not a good paternal example?

We have a hard time believing God wants a relationship with us. Some of us fight every step of the way.

And even if we do want a close relationship, how do we obtain it?

So what does the Bible say about God as father? Ephesians 4:6 reads, "One God and Father of all, who is over all and through all and in all." The Bible states He is a father to everyone. Including those who are hurt or have been hurt.

It took years for me to realize God our creator is also a God of love. Would a loving God want his children to be unhappy? Of course not. Only a hateful deity wants his daughters to live without joy. My God is not hateful. He is so full of love that He wants a personal relationship with each one of us.

God loves us and He created us to love Him back. In order to do so, He gave us free will to not love Him. When we finally say yes to Him, it means something more than just being a robot who loves on command or one who accepts as true out of fear.

Unlike some fathers who only gave their love when you did well in school or won the prize, God loves you no matter what you've done. And he loves all of us in spite of our faults.

If the foundation of God's love was my actions, I'd be in a lot of trouble. It's nice to know that no matter what I do, He'll never stop loving me. Or you. Unlike a pharisaical father, God's love is not based on who we are or what we've done. It's all because of who He is.

The best way to achieve the joy God has to offer is to ignore those shouts from the devil that claim God is just like dear old dad. For some of us, Dad wasn't very dear. However, our Heavenly Father is nothing but kind and forgiving. He never walks away to start another family. He's our paternal leader who is with us to the end of time.

No matter how far you ran from Him, He's always been right there beside you. He will never let go, and you can trust Him to be with you always.

Whether a believer or not, He wants a close relationship with us all. We can trust Him to be there with us when the going gets hard or when we mess up.

He's a loving father we can rely on.

God loves each of us as
if there is only one of us.
—*St. Augustine, philosopher*[iii]

Take Him at His Word

The sin underneath all our sins
is to trust the lie of the serpent
that we cannot trust the love and grace
of Christ and must take matters
into our own hands.
—*Martin Luther*[iv]

As stated in the introduction, most women have a list of things we dislike about ourselves. It doesn't always include just outward personifications. There are also inner thoughts that no one can see or hear.

This self-hate causes us to be insecure about who we are. We see our flaws as twice as big as others' imperfections. We look at their defects through a microscope while seeing ours through a magnifying glass. Because of how we view ourselves, the idea of being loved by God makes us warm and fuzzy, but also scared. We don't see ourselves the way God sees us.

At times, our words cut deeper than the loudest bully, and our opinions of ourselves lead us to judge ourselves as not good enough to be loved.

If we can't love ourselves, how can we expect anyone else to, much less God? In order to accept God's true joy, we must also accept that we are worthy of love. Not just His, but our own as well.

Society diminishes the role of women in the world. In some countries, women are still no more than property. However, God feels differently. We are His daughters. Nowhere in the Bible does God say women are inferior to men. In fact, Jesus treated women equal to men. He sat with them, dined with them, and spoke to them just as He did their male counterparts.

I'm going to let you on a little secret, ladies, I think sometimes God is happier with His daughters than His sons.

Why? Because women, at times, are more receptive to the message of Jesus Christ. We are willing to act upon that faith, sharing our belief in Jesus faster than some men.

We are also more willing to take God at verse value where men need to contemplate the Word. While men think on it, women act on it.

Maybe a wedge has come between you and Jesus. That divide could be something created because of pain or a sinful past. The evil one might be using friends or family members to attack you with words like, "I remember when you used to…". That's how the devil works, using those close to you to cause the most harm. You might feel as if there's a bull's-eye on your heart, and the world is using you for target practice.

Sometimes you might think God doesn't care about you. It will take time to realize God wants a relationship with you. This relationship began with Adam and Eve and grew into His love of coming to Earth in the form of a man named Jesus. Everything He did upon that cross was to grow closer to His children. To grow closer to you.

Yet some of us have trepidation when it comes to getting too close. A lot of that apprehension comes from our childhood. We judge God based on the actions of others. It's hard to trust when you grew up in a chaotic household.

My father was gone most of the time, working or drinking. We'd never know what kind of mood he'd come home in. The last thing I wanted was to worship an unpredictable God, who wants to call himself Father.

How can you accept God's love if you can't trust Him because of issues from your youth?

The first thing you need to do is realize you're not alone. Even people in the Bible had father issues.

In 1 Samuel 16, Samuel went to Jesse's home to find who God had anointed as the next king. He asked Jesse to bring all his sons out. Verses 16:10-11 reads, Jesse had seven of his sons pass before Samuel, but Samuel said to him, "'The Lord has not chosen these.' So he asked Jesse, 'Are these all the sons you have?' 'There is still the youngest,' Jesse answered. "He is tending the sheep.'"

Everything He did upon that cross
was to grow closer in a relationship
with His children.

Can you imagine how David felt when he discovered all his brothers were brought forward, yet he was left out in the fields? Jesse announced loud and clear he didn't think David was good enough to be king.

How many of you could never please your father? Nothing you did was ever good enough? A lot of us have our hands up. Well, for David, it only got worse. Once he was anointed to be king, he was brought to the castle where King Saul lived. The king grew jealous of David.

In 1 Samuel 18:10-11 Saul's anger shows through. "Now it came about on the next day that an evil spirit from God came mightily upon Saul, and he raved in the midst of the house, while David was playing the harp with his hand, as usual; and a spear was in Saul's hand. Saul hurled the spear for he thought, 'I will pin David to the wall.' But David escaped from his presence twice."

Can you imagine how David felt when Saul, who was probably like a surrogate father, tried to kill him?

Rejection can be like a slap in the face. It stings just as much. Tears well in your eyes in the same way. The only difference is instead of our cheek hurting, our hearts do.

Finding trust is never easy when you've been lied to, abused, or abandoned.

No matter how hard things got for David, he never forgot that God loved him. He was a man after God's own heart. Paul reminds us of this in Acts 13:22, "After removing Saul, he made David their king. God testified concerning him: 'I have found David son of Jesse, a man after my own heart; he will do everything I want him to do.'" David made mistakes, but his faith never wavered. Your faith mustn't either.

One of the best ways to trust that God is your one true father is to spend time in his Word. The more you study the Bible, the more you come to understand God and His love for you. Immerse yourself in positive verses about God's image. Verses like Titus 3: 4-6. "But when the kindness of God our Savior and His love for mankind appeared, He saved us, not on the basis of deeds which we have done in righteousness, but according to His mercy, by the washing of regeneration and renewing by the Holy Spirit, whom He poured out upon us richly through Jesus Christ our Savior."

Also look to other Christians. Those who feel God's joy. They're easy to recognize. They're the ones with tears flowing from their eyes every time God's grace and love are mentioned.

The more you see that joy rolling down their faces, the more you want what they have because you realize that love is real. It took years for me to accept that God loved me the same as He loved that tearful-eyed woman.

Don't allow what hurt you in the past to hold you in the past. You need to start each day with the notion that you are loved.

God's word proves it. Open the Bible and immerse yourself in his love daily.

We are children in God's eyes
and enjoy the special connection and love
only a father and his children can enjoy.
We are not just servants having a master,
but sons and daughters having a Father.
—John Servidio,
"God as a Father,"
LifeHopeandTruth.com[v]

Distorting "God as Father"

God is not someone who lives far away
in a place you can never reach.
Nor is he a heavenly warden,
eager to punish you for doing wrong.
He is a father who loves you.
He says to you:
I have loved you with an everlasting love,
so I am constant in my affection for you.
—Evansville Charismatic Renewal[vi]

Remember how your dad taught you to ride a bike? Maybe took you fishing? If you had a good dad, those are wonderful memories. There are a lot of wonderful things we associate with a father.

It's only natural someone who had a good dad could relate to God the Father as a wonderful deity. Chances are this good father went to church and taught you about the Lord. At the very least he showed you right from wrong and, in the ways he acted, showed that you were loved.

Unfortunately, there are those of us who did not have that type of relationship with their natural father. Because of this past relationship, any image of God as a father can become distorted.

When I hear an atheist scoff at God, especially if it's a female, my first thought is they had a bad relationship with their father. This distortion of God the Father is only going to get worse because today we live in a world of sperm donors. In our society, many girls come from broken homes where they rarely, if ever, see their biological father. Some have never known them at all. And then there are those girls who were not taken very good care of. Not just neglected and ignored, but abused by the one person who should have protected instead of causing pain.

Why is a father so important? Several studies have proven that fathers are needed to raise a boy to be a productive part of society. Most women are just not strong enough to raise a boy to be a man. However, fathers are just as important to their daughters as they are to their sons. Below are some of the reasons a good father is important to his daughter:

1. A good father will teach his daughter how she should be treated by men. If Dad treats Mom with respect, doesn't put down women for their appearance, and tells their daughters how beautiful and smart they are, girls will grow with good self-esteem. These fathers also set the bar higher when it comes to the men their daughters might date and marry.

2. If a loving father spends time with his daughter, he shows her she's important. However, if he's neglectful, he teaches his daughter that she doesn't matter. In time, she'll find men who use her and then move on.

3. A wonderful father can teach a girl how to respect herself.

Daughters without a good bond with their fathers may end up having sexual relationships at an early age; they could do poorly in school, or develop psychological problems like depression. They are more likely to turn to sex, drugs, or alcohol to fill the void inside.

4. Daughters with a good relationship with their fathers are less likely to commit suicide. Girls without fathers are five times more likely to kill themselves. The United States has an epidemic of suicidal teens. According to a USNews.com article, "Though the number of suicides among wom

en is highest among those who are middle-aged, girls ages 10 to 14 showed the highest percent increase, nearly tripling since 1999… Boys ages 10 to 14 showed the second-highest increase in suicide rates, though not reaching the same growth seen among females of the same age group."

5. Fathers teach women to trust. A father who is unpredictable, like mine, makes it hard to trust what you're seeing is real. A father can teach his daughter that actions speak louder than words. If he continually misses "dates" with her, she'll decide she isn't important to him and turn to men who are as neglectful as Dad.

Just how do you trust a God who wants to be close like a father when the one you had was neglectful or abusive, whether physically, emotionally, or sexually?

A father is supposed to keep you safe and make you feel secure. His choices might make it hard for you to trust anyone, much less a God who wants to be called Father. If you compare your spiritual Father to your natural dad, you might end up hating God.

First, let me say I understand where you're coming from. Like I said before, my dad was an alcoholic, and not a nice one like you see in the cartoons. At times our home was filled with verbal and/or physical abuse. It wasn't easy for me to come to faith and to love a god who wanted to be called Father. But once I accepted the love of Jesus, and studied scripture in the Bible, I realized God was nothing like my birth father.

God is loving and kind. He'll never put you down, abuse you, or abandon you.

There are several Bible verses which show proof of how much God cares about His children. A couple examples are 1 Peter 5:7 which reads,"Cast all your anxiety on him because he cares for you," and Nahum 1:7 reads, The Lord is good, a refuge in times of trouble. He cares for those who trust in him."

You may doubt the love of your birth father, but God's love is real. Realize that His love is everlasting as stated in Jeremiah 31:3, "The LORD appeared to him from afar, saying, "I have loved you with an everlasting love; Therefore I have drawn you with loving-kindness."" We are given plenty of this proof of God's love in the Bible. The best proof being that He came to Earth as a man to wash away our sins so we could spend eternity in Heaven. Does that sound like something an abusive father would do?

God should be respected,
but never feared to the point of terror.

We think of love as an emotion. An emotion is how we feel, but true love is really an action. Your husband might not tell you he loves you as often as you like, but he mows the lawn and keeps the house up. He proves his love by his actions.

The same is true of a loving father. He doesn't need to speak to show that he loves his daughter. He does so in the way he listens and gives her strength during her pain.

Some fathers taught their daughters how to drive. Unfortunately, there were those of us who were berated each time we stepped on the brake too hard or couldn't get the clutch in gear without that grinding noise. To this day, I won't attempt a vehicle with a stick shift because it reminds me of my father's anger. His actions told me

I was stupid because I couldn't drive a car with a manual gearshift.

Yet, God has never said I was stupid.

That's not to say God doesn't punish when we do wrong, but He will never leave scars whether emotional or physical. He works all times for our good. God should be respected, but never feared to the point of terror. His discipline is for our good. It is not out of some sadistic means of enjoyment.

What we see as discipline, at times, is just God allowing us to take responsibility for our own actions.

Charging a credit card can create debt and hardships. Not eating right causes weight gain and health issues. These are results of our own actions, not because our heavenly Father enjoys seeing us suffer. Our suffering could have been avoided if we'd only taken to heart one of God's favorite words – moderation.

Sometimes there are reasons God allows us to suffer through no fault of our own, but we'll get into that later in this book.

Even if you had a wonderful father, he had flaws. No matter how great he was, God is one hundred times better. But an abusive father or an absentee father, will be used by Satan to compromise your walk with Jesus. The evil one will use the comparison between your earthly father with your heavenly father to keep you from God's joy. There's nothing the devil hates more than a happy Christian, singing the praises of our King.

Still having trouble buying into that God the Father thing? Maybe you still believe you are unloved, read Romans 5:8, "but God shows his love for us in that while we were still sinners, Christ died for us." He came to Earth as a man and died for us. You and me.

There are Biblical references that prove God's love is more about action than emotion. For instance, if you feel abandoned, read Isaiah 41:10 – "So do not fear, for I am with you; do not be dismayed, for I am your God. I will strengthen you and help you; I will uphold you with my righteous right hand."

Do you feel like no one cares about you? Take a look at Jeremiah 29:11 where God tells us "'For I know the plans I have for you,' declares the LORD, 'plans to prosper you and not to harm you, plans to give you hope and a future.'"

Maybe you're just tired and in need of rejuvenation from all the world has tossed at you. If so, settle in with a cup of tea, relax, and see what Psalm 103:1-22 has to say. It's a bit too lengthy to put in the book, but trust me, it's worth a read when you need a good pick-me-up.

All these verses show God's love through actions.

God is not a spiritual version of your Earthly father. Your father might have left you, but God never will. Distorting the way you see God by comparing Him to your father only keeps Him at arm's length.

This distortion is the devil's twisted way to keep you from God's love. Any time you start to get that niggle in the back of your brain that says God is just like dear, old dad, remember God gave you the strength to get through your childhood. And He will be with you forever to get you through any other trials, holding you up when you need His support.

God's actions speak louder than any words. The minute you get up in the morning until you lay your head down at night, He shows you how much you are loved. Just look around. Is there a roof over your head? A car in the driveway? Food on the table? All these are examples of God's love.

We need to find a way to claim His love as our own.

In order to feel God's love, I stopped projecting my image of my drunken father onto God. I exchanged all my anger for love and joy. And you can do it too if you're willing to accept God's fatherly love through the verses He has to offer.

Life is hard and unfair.
It is cruel and heartless, painful,
trying, disappointing, unapologetic,
and frequently downright awful.
But that's not important.
What's important is that through it all
you learn how much you need
your Heavenly Father
and how much your friends need you.
—Richelle E. Goodrich,
author of
For Such As Time as This[ix]

Is He a Good, Good Father?

He watched over me before I knew him,
and before I learned sense
or even distinguished between good and evil,
and he protected me,
and consoled me
as a father would his son.
—Saint Patrick[x]

For a long time, I didn't think I was good enough to use the term Father when it came to God. I'd use Lord, telling myself I was showing respect. What I was actually doing was avoiding using anything that might remind me of the terrible relationship I had with my own dad. But the more I studied the Bible, the more I realized God wants us to call him Father. In Matthew 23:9, we are reminded to "call no man your father on earth, for you have one Father, who is in heaven."

Today, I'm jealous of people who use terms like "Daddy" or "Pappa" when it comes to God. It shows how their close relationship. I want that connection. How about you?

I still have plenty of steps to take before I experience that nearness, but it's something I'm willing to work for. That could be why He had me write this book. I'm a fiction writer, doing non-fiction isn't really my thing, but God works that way. He makes you think you're helping others when it's really helping you as well.

Without a close bond with their fathers, girls have a hard time getting near to God. They don't know what a deep relationship led by love feels like especially with a patriarchal figure. Yet they want something to fill that hole that's opened inside through a sense of abandonment.

Today, I'm jealous of people
who use terms like "Daddy" or "Pappa"
when it comes to God.
It shows how their close relationship.
I want that connection.
How about you?

Women like me long for that closeness of a fatherly relationship. Unfortunately, too many seek it in other men.

Men who abuse or abandon, like our fathers, can cause turmoil not only within the household but in their children's future as well. And even if we become saved, we still don't have that closeness with God that we want.

Below is a wonderful poem, from Jason Kirk Bartley, that gives full meaning to God the Father. I hope it touches you like it touched me.

Father of Light
by Jason Kirk Bartley

Father of light,
so perfect are thee.
I cannot hide.
Lord, be with me.
Father of light,
you love me so.
hold my hand,
never let go.
Father of light,
Your promises ring true.
This promise I make,
to be with you.
Father of light,
how you know all.
I'll be that Holy sacrifice,
fulfill your call.

God wants us to sense Him near us at all times so we will come running when He calls.

His love knows no bounds. Call Him Father, Daddy, or even Dad. All He really wants is for you to look on Him like a loving father, one you love as much as He loves you.

We believe in one God,
the Father Almighty,
Maker of heaven and earth,
and of all things visible and invisible;
and in one Lord Jesus Christ,
the only-begotten Son of God,
begotten of the Father before all worlds;
God of God, Light of Light,
very God of very God
—Nicene Creed[xii]

He Wants Your Love Also

When I consider Your heavens,
the work of Your fingers,
The moon and the stars,
which You have ordained;
What is man that You take thought of him,
And the son of man that You care for him?
—Psalm 8:3-4

This country has basically banished men from the title of fatherhood. There are dozens of television shows where the father is incompetent and can't do anything right. They come off like idiots while the mothers are the smart ones. I can't help but wonder if these women are so smart, why'd they marry someone so incompetent.

Society used to frown upon fathers who didn't take care of their children. Now the government pays so they don't have to. It's almost become the norm in some parts of this country. Is it any wonder boys are turning to gangs for the male leadership they need and girls turn to other men?

We've created a society of children who feel unwanted or unloved.

But God wants them. And He wants you. God loves you so much He thought you were worth dying for. He paid off our debt on the cross. And He gives us the gift of grace and forgiveness though we don't deserve it.

However, a father wants to know he's needed. God is no different. You can run, but He's right behind you. No matter how often you've walked away, He has never left you. He's determined to have a relationship with you. Isaiah 49:15-16 tells us, "Can a mother forget the baby at her breast and have no compassion on the child she has borne? Though she may forget, I will not forget you!" God has never forgotten any of us, no matter how far we've strayed.

God knows everything there is about you. Psalm 139:14 tells us "You have searched me, Lord, and you know me. You know when I sit and when I rise; you perceive my thoughts from afar. You discern my going out and my lying down; you are familiar with all my ways. Before a word is on my tongue you, Lord, know it completely." And even though we sin, He still wants a relationship with us. He wants to be the place we run in times of trouble, like a good, good father. Psalm 46:1 reminds us " . . . God is our refuge and strength, an ever-present help in trouble."

When you live in a home where you were abandoned by your father whether physically or emotionally, go to a school where you're a social outcast, you turn to something to fill that void inside. For me, it was alcohol. For others, it might be drugs or sex with a variety of partners. No one is around to tell us God loves us. And if they try, we scoff, thinking He's no better than the man we call Dad. Yet God is the only thing that can fill the hole we have inside. No amount of shopping can end that pain. Only the love of Jesus Christ can fill us with the joy we desire.

No matter what you've been through,
God can work good from it
if you'll allow Him the opportunity.

We are valuable in God's eyes.

Your feelings might be saying I can't forget what was done to me. Your flesh might even burn at the notion. But your heart needs to risk that only God's love is real and true, and only He can take away the pain.

Humans want to be not only loved but to belong. God is there to listen and be the father we needed years ago. We belong with Him.

Sit next to God, tell Him your story. No matter what you've been through, God can work good from it if you'll allow Him the opportunity.

And no matter how far you stray, He will look for you. That is how much you are worth. In Luke 15, Jesus tells the parable of the lost sheep. A shepherd will search everywhere for one sheep who has wandered off. In verse 15:7, Jesus states, "I tell you that in the same way there will be more rejoicing in heaven over one sinner who repents than over ninety-nine righteous persons who do not need to repent." God will spend your life trying to get you to come home.

Below is an acrostic that might help you more clearly see proof of God's love:

F = Faithful: 1 Corinthians 1:9: "God is faithful, who has called you into fellowship with his Son, Jesus Christ our Lord."

A = Approachable: Matthew 11:28: "Come to me, all you who are weary and burdened, and I will give you rest."

T = Trustworthy: Psalm 28:7: "The Lord is my strength and my shield; My heart trusts in Him, and I am helped; Therefore my heart exults, And with my song I shall thank Him."

H = Hope: Romans 15:13: "May the God of hope fill you with all joy and peace as you trust in him, so that you may overflow with hope by the power of the Holy Spirit."

E = Eternal: Psalm 90:2: "Before the mountains were born or you brought forth the earth and the world, from everlasting to everlasting you are God."

R = Reliable: Psalm 18:2: "The Lord is my rock, my fortress and my deliverer; my God is my rock, in whom I take refuge, my shield and the horn of my salvation, my stronghold."

Still need more proof God wants to be your father? Let's take a look at the Lord's prayer. In Mathew 6, Jesus explains the proper way to pray. In verses 9-13, Jesus said, "This, then, is how you should pray:

> Our Father in heaven,
> hallowed be your name,
> your kingdom come,
> your will be done,
> on earth as it is in heaven.
> Give us today our daily bread.
> And forgive us our debts,
> as we also have forgiven our debtors.
> And lead us not into temptation,
> but deliver us from the evil one.

The first line says it, "Our Father in Heaven." This line alone allows us to take ownership of God as our father. Later we learn that He "gives us," "forgives us," "leads us," and "delivers us." These are all ways He shows He's a loving father.

Pray this prayer as you end this chapter. Recognize how He loves you. Once you do, it should give the Lord's Prayer a deeper meaning.

The more you come to realize God's love for you, the less you'll rely on those emotions that keep you tangled up in knots. But in order to have a close relationship with Him, you must see yourself through God's eyes, not as a reflection of what is in the mirror or in your past.

> The more I contemplate God,
> the more God looks on me.
> The more I pray to him,
> the more he thinks of me too.
> —Bernard of Clairvaux[xiii]

To Dig Deeper

A. Here are some questions to help you dig a bit deeper into your relationship with God.

1. When you think of a father, what comes to mind? Did a lot of what you came up with have to do with your relationship with your own father? How do you feel when you think of God the Father?

2. Put down the worst experience you ever had with your father or father figure. Now list the best. How did that make you feel as opposed to the worst experience? Which story have you related the most to other people? Why?

3. Most Christians know John 3:16 states, "For God so loved the world that he gave his one and only Son, that whoever believes in him shall not perish but have eternal life." We hear that verse so much that some of us say it without the emotion it deserves. But we seldom read the verse that follows. 3:17 continues with, "For God did not send His Son into the world to condemn the world, but to save the world through Him." How does this additional verse make you feel?

4. A lot of women who grow up without the emotional support of a father ultimately will turn to something else to fill that emptiness. Sex, drugs, shopping, and food are some of the ways we fill this void. Can you name other ways in which we fill that hole in our hearts? How do you any hole you have? Now that you know this is a "crutch" for you, how can you adjust your habits to fill the emptiness inside another way?

5. I did an acrostic of the word FATHER above. Do your own.

F =
A =
T =
H =
E =
R =

6. If you didn't pray the Lord's prayer above, do so now. Now say it again, only exchange the words "Our Father" for "My Father." Does this change bring you a bit closer to God?

7. Below is a list of several different names God has been referred to, along with their meanings. Which one gives you the deepest emotional reaction? Repeat the Lord's prayer above, only this time instead of saying "Our Father," use whatever description you chose below.

El Shaddai - God Almighty
El Elyon - God Most High
El Olam - Everlasting God
El Roi - The God who Sees
Yahweh Bore - The Lord Creator
Yahweh Rapha - The Healing Lord
Yahweh Yireh - The Lord Will Provide

B: Read the following Bible verses. Reflect on them. How does each show God's love for you?

1. John 14:1-2: "Do not let your hearts be troubled. Trust in God; trust also in me. In my Father's house are many rooms; if it were not so, I would have told you. I am going there to prepare a place for you."

   a. How does it feel to know God has prepared a place for you in His house?

   b. Time to use your imagination. Close your eyes and picture

God's house. What does it look like? What colors are used? What is the most comfortable piece of furniture? What is your favorite room?

2. Romans 8:37-39: "No, in all these things we are more than conquerors through him who loved us. For I am convinced that neither death nor life, neither angels nor demons, neither the present nor the future, nor any powers, neither height nor depth, nor anything else in all creation, will be able to separate us from the love of God that is in Christ Jesus our Lord."

a. Most of us, if we're parents, would never stop loving our child, no matter what they did. How does it make you feel to know God's love is just as deep?

b. As stated in this verse, you will never be separated from God's love in the present or the future. Why do you think this verse didn't say "past?"

3. Romans 8:15-17: "For you did not receive the spirit of slavery to fall back into fear, but you have received the Spirit of adoption as sons, by whom we cry, "Abba! Father!" The Spirit himself bears witness with our spirit that we are children of God, and if children, then heirs—heirs of God and fellow heirs with Christ, ..."
a. This verse talks about how you were adopted and are now an heir to God. What type of "beneficiary" share do you most look forward to?

b: A lot of people who believe in a higher being have somewhat of a master/slave relationship. Basically, do as I say or you will be punished. Jesus Christ wants to have a loving relationship with us. God wants us to look on him like a father. Why do you think so many seem to want the master/slave over the father/child?
4. 1 John 4:9-11: "This is how God showed his love among us: He sent his one and only Son into the world that we might live through him. This is love: not that we loved God, but that he

loved us and sent his Son as an atoning sacrifice for our sins. Dear friends, since God so loved us, we also ought to love one another."

a. The last part of this states we are to "love one another." Send someone a note letting them know why you love them. Now write down or tell someone something you like about yourself. Which was easier? Why do you think that is?

b. God showed His love by sacrificing Himself on the cross for our sins. Have you ever sacrificed something for another? Did they realize it? Did they appreciate all you did for them?

5. Ephesians 3:17-19: "… And I pray that you, being rooted and established in love, may have power, together with all the Lord's holy people, to grasp how wide and long and high and deep is the love of Christ, and to know this love that surpasses knowledge—that you may be filled to the measure of all the fullness of God."

a. Close your eyes again and picture yourself breathing in the fullness of God. How does that feel? Now picture yourself being rooted to the ground beside a marker that says "Love." Which picture gave you greater joy?

b. Women have a tendency to think they need to lose weight all the time. We listen to the scale way too much. However, instead of seeing ourselves as overweight, what if we saw ourselves as full of God? Would that make a difference as to how you feel about yourself and your weight?

CHAPTER TWO
Someone Like Me

*If I could change one thing about myself,
it would be the voices in my head.
They don't like me.*
—*Pink, Singer and Songwriter*[xiv]

How many times have you ever looked in the mirror and said, "I'm fat" or "I'm ugly?" After making a mistake at work or school, how often have you mumbled, "I'm stupid," or thought, "I'll never be good enough?"

Fathers are so important to a daughter's self-esteem. A father should be there to help her learn to like herself and build confidence. Girls who don't have a good male role model at home are likely to look elsewhere for the assurance they need, including the arms of older men.

The hardest part of accepting God's love is in believing we are worthy of that love especially if our fathers never showed us any.

We grow up used to having self-hate, constantly berating ourselves or listening to others tear us down. As stated earlier, girls who grow up in fatherless homes are more likely to end up suffering from depression. They lack self-confidence in themselves and their attributes.

While most Christian women believe the Lord cares, some have never truly felt that deep affection He has to offer. How can Jesus love and accept someone like me? These three little words are used by women every day all over the world.

Someone like me.

Never said with a smile or with love, but with disdain. We see ourselves as imperfect, flawed, and broken. There isn't one woman who doesn't have something about her outer being she'd like adjusting (weight, wrinkles), or in her past that she doesn't wish she could change.

Be reassured, it doesn't matter how bad you think your sin was or is, God still loves you.

In John 8:1-11, while Jesus was at the temple, a group of men tossed a woman down at His feet. She'd been caught in the act of adultery. The men tried to get Jesus to say she should be stoned, instead, He said for the man who has not sinned to throw the first rock. Of course, no one could. Once all the men had left, Jesus turned to the woman. In verses 10-11, He said to her, "…'Where are your accusers? Didn't even one of them condemn you?' 'No, Lord,' she said. And Jesus said, 'Neither do I. Go and sin no more.'"

She was caught in the act and these men tossed her at Jesus' feet. Ignore right now that the man she was having the affair with wasn't brought forward. Look at what Jesus said to her instead. She was forgiven. The Bible doesn't tell us what happened to this woman, but I'll bet his kindness had an impact on her.

You are a wonderful being in Christ,
so cast away those feelings of self-doubt.
See yourself through His eyes.

No matter what you did fifteen years ago, fifteen days ago, or even fifteen minutes ago, your sins are forgiven. Your past is not who you are. Starting today, you need to see yourself as a daughter to God.

Don't let the devil tell you otherwise. Satan would like nothing more than to take you way from God. The larger a wedge he can drive between you and the Father, the happier the evil one becomes.

Nothing makes the devil angrier than a woman who basks in God's glory. With Jesus she can do anything.

Today is the day to sit up tall and take God's love for your own. Let His light shine so bright in you that it blinds those around who are trying to keep you down. Show the world the glory of a God tan.

All it takes is fixing what's broken inside. It's just that easy. And that difficult.

The good news is, with Jesus, you can do just that. In Ephesians 4:22-24 we're told, "You were taught, with regard to your former way of life, to put off your old self, which is being corrupted by its deceitful desires;to be made new in the attitude of your minds; and to put on the new self, created to be like God in true righteousness and holiness." Made over with a new attitude means you not only stop from committing sin, but you stop hating yourself.

Your sins of the past are wiped clean in God's eyes through the blood of Jesus Christ. It doesn't matter if you were a thief, a liar, or a prostitute. And it wasn't your fault your biological father abandoned you or abused you. That was his issue, not yours.

You are a wonderful being in Christ, so cast away those feelings of self-doubt. See yourself through His eyes.

The next time you say those three words, someone like me, do so with a smile on your face because God certainly does love someone like you.

Society may say
you don't fit the beauty mold,
but God looks at you and smiles,
knowing that He created you
just the way He wanted
—Grace Houle[xvi]

Voices in Your Head

Time heals all wounds.
And if it doesn't,
you name them something
other than wounds
and agree to let them stay.
—Emma Forrest,
author of
Does My Soul Look Big in This?[xvii]

———————

Have you ever been somewhere and heard your Mom's voice in your head? Maybe she was the one who told you to always smile or to not talk to strangers. These momisms stick with us most of our lives. Eventually, we hear ourselves using the same words with our own daughters.

But there's also another voice we hear. The one that undermines our self-confidence. The ones that tell you you're no good. I hear them all the time. The big one – you're fat! I hate it because, no matter how good I feel about myself, I still see that fat kid in the mirror I grew up with.

God sees us differently. He looks at our hearts, not the outward appearance that society deems important. Just read the Bible for proof.

Isaiah 43:4 tells us that "Since you are precious and honored in my sight, and because I love you, ..." you are beautiful. 1 John 1:19, "If we confess our sins, he is faithful and just to forgive us our sins and to cleanse us from all unrighteousness." This lets us know we are forgiven. And John 3:16,"For God so loved the world, that he gave his only Son, that whoever believes in him should not perish but have eternal life" shows how much God loves you.

Each time a negative thought pops in, we must drive it out with something positive.

One way to do that is to make a list of these negative thoughts then go to the Bible for God's truth. Below are some of my issues.

My Views: I had a child out of wedlock. I'm no good.
God's Words: You are forgiven
(Isaiah 43:25: "I, even I, am he who blots out your transgressions, for my own sake, and remembers your sin no more.)

My Views: I'm not that smart.
God's Words: You have gifts to use in My name
(1 Peter 4:10: "Each of you should use whatever gift you have received to serve others, as faithful stewards of God's grace in its various forms.")

My Views: I'm fat and ugly.
God's Words: I made you in my image. Am I ugly?
(Genesis 1:27: "So God created mankind in his own image, in the image of God he created them; male and female he created them.")

My Views: Why can't I get out of this rut? I'm such a loser.
God's Words: I have plans for you. Be patient.
(Jeremiah 29:11: "For I know the plans I have for you," declares the LORD, "plans to prosper you and not to harm you, plans to give you hope and a future.")

As you can see, God can deal with any hateful words I use against myself. He can do the same for you.

When you're down, and you need comfort, remember Revelations 21:4: "He will wipe every tear from their eyes. There will be no more death or mourning or crying or pain, for the old order of things has passed away." Our Godly Father cares enough to take away our pain.

Pray for God to show you where you excel so you can focus more on those good qualities than what you perceive to be your imperfections. And ask Him to show you where He wants you to improve. Don't be surprised if He doesn't mention the flaws you've got stuck in your head.

Let go of those words of self-hate that keep you down. Your past is over. You are a new creation.

Psalm 103:12 reads, "As far as the east is from the west, so far has He removed our transgressions from us." How much does Jesus love you? From one outstretched hand to the other. Never forget a love so deep He died for you upon that cross. He gave us a torn veil and a way into the kingdom. We just need to take the path He's provided.

God considers each of us His favorite child. We are all daughters of the one true King, and He wants nothing more than for you to take his hand in confidence.

Too many of us wait to come to Jesus with excuses like "I'll go to church when…," or "I'm just not good enough, yet." Only one person who walked this Earth was perfect. Jesus. He showed us how to live an almost impossible life, yet when we became a Christian, for some reason we expected to become sin-free. And when it doesn't happen, we forget all about God's grace.

Once you get it in your mind
that the evil one is lying to you
whenever you allow self-hate in,
God's love becomes more real.

Ask any Christian if they can remember how easy it was when they first came to Jesus. Don't be surprised by the laughter. Most of us have stories of strife, family members turning against us, etc.

The same will be true when you take this deep journey to take God as your father. The devil will come at you with full force. He'll bring up your past hurts or current sins, anything to keep you from God's arms. And most of his attacks will come from your friends and family as well, so be prepared. The evil one doesn't want you to forget how you were hurt as a child or how you dislike yourself.

We all struggle with the idea that God loves us unconditionally. People have a tendency to conceptualize God and His love for them.

We put it in human form where there are conditions. But God has no conditions. We expect there to be a catch. But with God there is none. All we have to do to get God's love is to accept it. His love cannot be earned, it came at the price of Jesus' death and resurrection.

As if I didn't live with rejection and self-doubt enough as a kid, God made me an author. Me - Ms. Grammatically-challenged. There is nothing more challenging for someone who felt abandoned as a child than to be a writer as an adult. Not a week goes by I don't get rejected by an agent, a publisher, or a reader. That voice in my head will scream "Loser!" louder than anyone else's. How can I sense God's love with all that?

I listen to Christian music from bands like Disciple and Kutless. And I pray.

Once you get it in your mind that the evil one is lying to you whenever you allow self-hate in, God's love becomes more real.

When your mind gets it, your heart will shortly follow. But, it takes time spent with the Bible and other Christians in order to come to this realization.

You don't have to be perfect to be loved by Jesus. He didn't hang with perfect people. In fact, those who thought they were better, He wanted nothing to do with. Jesus went to the poor, the sinners, the imperfect. As proof, look to Mark 2:15-17, When Jesus was having dinner at Levi's house along beside tax collectors and sinners, the teachers of the law asked his disciples: "'Why does he eat with tax collectors and sinners? On hearing this, Jesus said to them, "It is not the healthy who need a doctor, but the sick. I have not come to call the righteous, but sinners.'"

In biblical times, tax collectors were considered the lowest of the lows. Most were very abusive and thieves. Yet, here, Jesus was not only speaking with them but dining with them.

The Pharisees were disgusted that He hung out with sinners.

Some of us look at ourselves as not good enough to claim God as Father because of our pasts. But, like a loving father, God might not like your actions, but He's never stopped loving you. Your sin was no surprise to God. He knew you would run from Him before you did. But, no matter how far you went, He has always been there with you, and He is there, ready to accept you back. He's never stopped loving His daughter.

One of my favorite verses of the Bible is Psalm 91:4. It reads, "He will cover you with his feathers, and under his wings you will find refuge; his faithfulness will be your shield and rampart." What a great visual. Don't allow your past hurts to conform you, allow them to transform you into God's daughter.

We see our flaws, the wrinkles, dents, and cottage cheese thighs. We suffer from inner pain and hide our sins deep inside, but God sees our hearts. If we allow this transformation, He can breathe us back to life.

Once you accept God's love totally, you go from being a mess to being calm, not caring about your past. You walk around with a smile because you're filled with the freedom God has to offer. 2 Corinthians 3:17 states "Now the Lord is the Spirit, and where the Spirit of the Lord is, there is freedom." Freedom from your past pain. Freedom to experience love, no matter who you are. The freedom of grace and forgiveness.

He doesn't love you one day and not the next. James 1:17 reminds us, "Every good and perfect gift is from above, coming down from the Father of the heavenly lights, who does not change like shifting shadows." Jesus meets you right here, right now, in your current circumstances. There's no need to be perfect.

Push those voices out with positive words. Keep God at the forefront of your mind and the freedom from all those negative thoughts can be yours.

Unless we form the habit
of going to the Bible
in bright moments as well as in trouble,
we cannot fully respond to its consolations
because we lack equilibrium
between light and darkness.
—*Helen Keller*[xviii]

Feeling God's Love Through Our Emotions

I have been driven many times
upon my knees by the overwhelming conviction
that I had nowhere else to go.
My own wisdom and that of all about me
seemed insufficient for that day.
—*Abraham Lincoln*[xix]

We've all heard stories of kids sitting by the window waiting for their dad to show up for his weekend visit, and he never comes. Sad circumstances, and far more of this today than decades ago.

Humans want a close relationship with others. As children, that was our parents. As we grow, we desire an intimate relationship with some being higher than we are. That's why most cultures worship something other than themselves. The Greeks had mythology, there's Buddhism, Hinduism, etc. We want to know there is something bigger out there than just us.

It's a scary thought to think we are the best there is.

For Christians, that belief of course, is in Jesus Christ, our Lord and Savior. As such, we want some sort of connection with God. Some days we get that connection. That euphoria of experiencing His presence, His joy surrounds us.

Other times we can't feel Him near, and we think we've been left alone to deal with our circumstances. It's the same emptiness as when Dad never showed up.

At these times, we think God has turned against us, or worse, there is no God, and we were just fooling ourselves by believing in the first place.

It's easy to feel His presence when others are around, shouting His joys. A lot harder when we're alone during a bad situation. But, God is a constant in our lives. His promise to be here with us always are true. Deuteronomy 31:6 says, "… the Lord your God goes with you; he will never leave you nor forsake you."

Yet at these emotionally charged times, you might believe He has abandoned you.

Just because you don't think Jesus is beside you, doesn't mean he isn't. It doesn't matter if you are a Christian, atheist, or a Muslim. That whisper in your ear saying "Don't do that," is Him.

Childhood abandonment issues perpetuate those views that God has left you. You trusted Dad and look how he let you down. Can God be any different?

Consider whether your situation might be creating the illusion of God's rejection. Maybe your child is sick, or a parent received a terrible prognosis from the doctor. At these times, it's harder to feel God's presence because your world is in a state of disarray. You might not hear God because you've had a long day, not because he's not speaking to you.

At these times,
we have to ignore our feelings
and go with what we know is the truth.
God is with us, and He loves us.

If you have taken a step back and reviewed your situation and you still don't feel God near, there are things you can do to not feel so alone.

1. One is to talk with your church sisters. Have them pray with you and for you;

2. Recall where you were when you last felt God's presence. If at church, review the sermon, listen to the music that was played. I usually experience God's nearness during a certain Christian song. In order to get that sensation again, I pull that song up on the computer. Whatever it was that can return you to that state of passion for God, use it.

3. Intentionally focus on Jesus. We get so busy with our lives, we

have a tendency to put Him last on our list. He wants to be first.

4. Finally, focus on your blessings. Are you hungry? Then God's provided you with food. Are you warm in the winter, cool in the summer? A/C and heat are gifts from God. How about the beauty outside your window – flowers, trees, etc.? These are blessings from God to make you happy. Everything from the shoes on your feet to the blue sky above are gifts from God that show His love for you.

The above steps should help you get back in touch with God. If not, it might have more to do with our situation than the fact He's not listening.

We need to stop looking at God through our emotions. His love is a constant love, not an emotional love. Instead, see Him through your mind not your pain and hurt.

Another reason we don't hear is because we don't listen. Could He be telling you "no" regarding a situation, but you don't want to hear it. We ignore Him all the time in the hopes He changes His mind, just like a teenager does to a parent.

When we're alone and hurting, we have a tendency to focus on ourselves and our own pain, whether emotional or physical. It's hard to find God when you're being self-absorbed with our own issues. Change the focus of your attention from your situation to your loving Father. Pray to Him. Fall down on your knees. Picture Him folding His arms around you and taking you against His chest, holding you like a loving father would.

At times when you feel abandoned by God, ignore your emotions and go with your mind instead. Not those voices that berate you, but the truth you've read in the Bible. God is with you, and He loves you. It's hard, but you need to believe in His love even when you don't feel it.

Feelings are inconsistent. One minute we're high, the next low — all in one Budweiser Clydesdale commercial break. Satan uses our emotions to hold us hostage in order to keep us from our loving Father. Realizing this is a game of the evil one will make it easier to take a step back and re-evaluate the situation.

And don't allow cruel words to slip into your mind. Words like, He doesn't care.

Look around. See where He has shown His love in many ways throughout your life.

For some reason, we listen for Him to speak to us in a thunderous voice booming from above, but His tone is usually soft and quiet. In most cases, we need peace in order to hear Him. Find a quiet place where you can listen intently. He also might speak through someone close to you. He could be using them as a proxy, so be receptive of any friend stopping by.

If your mind starts to play tricks on you, saying things like "God doesn't care," or "Why would He allow this to occur," you need to reevaluate the situation. And remember these words are from Satan. Be on guard when the evil one uses our emotional state to create doubt in your faith and your heavenly Father.

The deeper you get into the Word, the closer you will feel to God. And tell others what you're going through. Sharing will help free some of that doubt. Matthew 18:20 states, "For where two or three gather in my name, there am I with them."

It's not easy, but we need to stop projecting our views of inadequacy and loneliness on God.

As long as we remember He has always been there and always will be, these abandonment issues will lessen. Eventually you will feel the return of His presence and hear His voice loud and clear.

God designed your emotion
to be gauges,
not guides.
—*Jon Bloom*[xx]

Unplanned Means Unwanted

Quit criticizing what God has created
Every time we do that
it's like we're turning our back
on what God thinks of us.
—*Marcia Greenwood*[xxi]

There is nothing better than being a mom. Okay, maybe being a grandmother. But, as a new mom, you get to plan for the baby. Things such as color choices for the nursery, names for your child, and so on. All the things that go into having a child that are fun.

However, a lot of kids these days are born out of wedlock. Their parents don't plan for them. Sometimes they don't even want them to the point they have an abortion. Those that end up keeping the child, and remain unmarried, in most cases, the mother ends up raising the child with very little help from the father, whether monetarily or physically. A lot of times he's off creating another life with another woman.

That doesn't mean you can't still enjoy some of the fun, but there are a lot more hardships involved. And even if you are married, the woman could find herself alone to deal with the issue of being a single mother through divorce.

I was both these women. With my first child, I wasn't married. However, my situation turned out to be a blessing. I wasn't going down a good path, drinking heavily, smoking marijuana, starting to take pills. Once I discovered I was pregnant, I quit all that. In essence, my child saved my life. And while she was unplanned, she's never been unwanted.

My second daughter was planned, and I was married at the time. However, the marriage ended in divorce when she was a toddler. He worked out of town four months at a time, home for only two, so in essence, I raised the children by myself. Not always easy since I had to deal with all the school and health issues.

Most single mothers can relate. I'm lucky because my ex-husband loves both of the children. He even adopted my oldest. He's always supported them monetarily, and he's made a point of spending time with them when he was in town.

However, there are those children whose fathers refuse to acknowledge them. This leaves a feeling of being unloved and unwanted.

Women who grew up with rejection have a tendency to be rebellious against a higher authority. We live with the belief that if I got through my childhood without help, I can make it the rest of the way. That works until something devastating occurs. A child gets very ill or a close friend dies unexpectedly. In our time of need, we find ourselves alone with nothing to turn to - no higher power to cling to for hope. That loneliness is the worst emotion in the world. A black hole of darkness where you keep spinning with no way to stop.

Like a lot of women these days, I never felt important to my father. At one time, I believed it was because he wasn't there when I was born. He was a State Representative for Idaho and was away at the time of my birth. I was the only birth he wasn't in the waiting room for. (In those days, dads weren't allowed in the birthing room.) When I discovered this, it made me believe I wasn't loved. Everyone else was more important.

I'm not alone. My generation is full of women raising children created by men who pretend to care but are only giving lip service. They flit from one woman to another creating life and then walk away. And these children end up feeling like they don't matter.

While your parents might not have planned for you, God did.

It doesn't matter how your story read in the past, you shouldn't allow one chapter to define the entire book. I don't want to hear any more this I was unplanned, so I was unloved stuff. God loved you and still does, even if no one else did. (But I assume there were others as well if you look back. Maybe grandparents or aunts or uncles.)

Our heavenly Father doesn't like it when we say bad things like I don't matter. You are precious to Him. Psalm 139:13, says, "For you created my inmost being; you knit me together in my mother's womb." You are a wondrous creation, knitted together by our God. And while you might have been a shock for your parents, God planned for you to come into this world.

Your mother probably also dreamt of what you would become with your life. But God saw your future. You see, Jeremiah 29:11 states, "'For I know the plans I have for you,' declares the Lord, 'plans to prosper you and not to harm you, plans to give you hope and a future.'" He has a plan for all His children, even those not expected by their parents.

It doesn't matter
how your story read in the past,
you shouldn't allow one chapter
to define the entire book.

You were not an accident in God's eyes. He not only planned for you, but He created you in His image. And your heavenly Father chose every part of you, from your skin color to the hairs on your head. Luke 12:7 says, "Indeed, the very hairs of your head are all numbered…" You are so important to God that He knows how many hairs are on your head. Can you say that about any of your children?

Before the doctor gave your mother a sonogram, your heavenly Father saw you. Psalm 139:16 reads, "Your eyes saw my unformed body; all the days ordained for me were written in your book before one of them came to be."

It doesn't matter if you were unplanned by your parents, you were never unplanned by God. He's always walked beside you. Ephesians 1:4 reminds us that "he chose us in him before the creation of the world to be holy and blameless in his sight."

Unfortunately, in our society, fatherlessness is a growing epidemic, so more children are growing up believing they are unloved. That rejection follows them into adulthood.

It's not easy to live feeling unloved, but Rejection is nothing new. Take Leah in Genesis 29-31. Jacob fell in love with her sister,

Rachel. He worked seven years in order to marry her. However, on the night of his marriage, he discovered he'd been tricked. Leah had been put in place of her sister.

Imagine how rejected Leah must have felt being forced to marry a man who didn't want her. When Jacob found out, I'm sure he must have been angry. I can't help but wonder if he took some of that anger out on her. Not necessarily physically, but he probably didn't think too much about what she was going through.

Most women today don't have to worry about being given to a man they don't love, like Leah. However, a father walking out can be just as painful as one who shows a lack of concern by giving you to a man who doesn't want you.

God will never give you away like Leah's father did with her. You are His, and He wants you to be happy. So, whenever you look in the mirror, take a moment to really look at yourself. See the perfect love you are in God's eyes.

Look at the beauty that is you. You are His creation. You are His daughter.

———————

You are not what others think you are.
You are what God knows you are.
—Shannon Alder,
Author of
*300 Questions to Ask Parents
Before It's Too Late*[xxii]

———————

If God Loves Me, Why Do I Hurt?

Our hurts
can become the very places
where we meet God
and experience the intimacy
of his comforting presence.
—Leigh McLeroy[xxiii]

———————

According to Victimsofcrime.org, One in five girls and one in ten boys are sexually assaulted each year. And according to the National Cancer Institute, while cancer is rare among children, "it is the leading cause of death by disease past infancy among children in the United States."

A lot of people wonder how a loving God could allow a child to get cancer or to be sexually abused. It's a good question asked by Christians daily.

Is it karma? Did we do something bad and are now being punished? What good is a God who walks away when you need him most? The more you contemplate this, the more you'll sense a deep loss, like He doesn't love you anymore.

Earthquakes, terrorism, tornadoes, and children who die. It's hard to believe God is really a good, good father when you see these tragedies hit. He can stop them but chooses not to. Why would a loving father allow such things to occur to his children?

When everything is fine in your life, your belief can be strong. It's during a time of extreme pressure that your faith is truly tested. If you don't have a strong foundation in Jesus to begin with, your faith could disappear altogether leaving you to believe God never really existed. However, it wasn't really God you were relying on. It was the calm life you were living at that particular moment.

Doubt is a tool Satan uses to keep you from the joy of knowing God's love. It's a voice that whispers in the back of your mind "He doesn't love you anymore" or "How can God let this happen?" Doubt also makes us think we are less of a Christian. It not only attacks our faith, it goes after our parenting ability, our job skills and other aspects of our lives. Any way the devil can sneak in and keep you from having true happiness, he will.

No one really knows why some things occur, but God does have a reason.

The best way through any type of emotional pain is to turn to your heavenly Father. 2 Corinthians 1:3-4 states we should "Praise be to the God and Father of our Lord Jesus Christ, the Father of compassion and the God of all comfort, who comforts us in all our troubles, so that we can comfort those in any trouble with the comfort we ourselves receive from God."

By suffering, you can help others with the same issues. It's God's way of molding us into His creation so later we can do His bidding. If you never lost a child, how can you relate to someone who has? If you hadn't had breast cancer, how can you tell other survivors that you know what they are going through?

He wants us to be able to help others later. It's usually easier to do so if you can relate to what someone is going through. For some of us, we believe our scars are God's ways of showing anger. You couldn't be more wrong. They are really stories for you to tell others and help them through. He may let you be wounded, but he'll mend you in the end.

He's also given us free will. Unfortunately, for some of us, we are having to live a harsh life because of the sins of our father. Don't get me wrong. There is evil in the world that you have no control over. But that's another problem with free will. These are choices people make that harm others. But don't think they will get away with it forever. Psalm 37:10 warns those who do evil that "A little while, and the wicked will be no more; though you look for them, they will not be found."

By suffering,
you can help others with the same issues.
It's God's way of molding us
into His creation
so later we can do His bidding.

We also have to live with the consequences of our own choices. We blame God when the roof caves in on us, and we have no money to repair it. Yet it was our choice to purchase a house we couldn't afford.

That's a problem we face with free will, even those who are not doing evil. We have to live with the repercussions of bad choices. That doesn't make God a bad father. That is a father who is teaching us right from wrong and to live within our limits. A good father loves but also disciplines. He'll listen to you complain but he'll also let you live with the consequences of your actions. God loves us through everything. He doesn't want us to suffer, but because of Adam & Eve there's disease and sin. We could be living in Heaven, but because of our sins, we suffer.

2 Peter 3:13 informs us that things will be different in Heaven. "But in keeping with his promise we are looking forward to a new heaven and a new earth, where righteousness dwells." There will be joy and singing for the Lord.

At difficult times, you must totally saturate your days with Jesus until you realize how special you are to Him. And you are special. He died for you. Yes, YOU. If that doesn't say love, nothing does.

Another thing tragedies do is build character. It's hard to understand how God, who wants to be called Father, allows us to go through pain. If He cares, why doesn't He just take it away? The Bible at Romans 5:3-5 actually says tribulation develops character. "And not only this, but we also exult in our tribulations, knowing that tribulation brings about perseverance; and perseverance, proven character; and proven character, hope; and hope does not disappoint because the love of God has been poured out within our hearts through the Holy Spirit who was given to us." Though it may not seem like it, by suffering, we become stronger in our faith.

How do you trust someone who allows you to be hurt? It's a great question, and one of our toughest dilemmas with God.

But, He never promised us that life would be a walk in the park. There will be trials. There will be heartbreak. That's part of life here on earth. However, He did promise to be with us during our struggles.

If you don't have a strong foundation
in Jesus to begin with,
your faith could disappear altogether
leaving you to believe God
never really existed.

And Jesus knows that pain of loss. He needed time alone after hearing about the death of John the Baptist, his cousin. In Matthew 14:13, it says "… he withdrew by boat privately to a solitary place." He knew that deep pain of losing someone He cared for.

And don't forget God had to watch as this world put His son to death on the cross.

You are never alone, God is with you. Always. Keep your eyes focused on the Lord. Seek God before a crisis occurs then it'll be natural to go to Him when something bad happens. He knows you, so rely on Him to comfort you.

Know that no matter how many times you ask, "Why, God? Why?" There is a reason. And there is a happy ending in Heaven. 1 Peter 5:10 says, "And the God of all grace, who called you to his eternal glory in Christ, after you have suffered a little while, will himself restore you and make you strong, firm and steadfast." Isn't it nice to know that God will make you strong again, and He will take away your pain? It might not be in this realm, but it will definitely be in Heaven.

During your lifetime, you might never understand why God put you through such misery, but in the end, it will become clear.

I know it's not easy to look to God when He has allowed you to live through something tragic, but it will add peace to your suffering. And there were those in the Bible who also felt that deep pain. People like David who lost a child. There was Ruth who lost a husband and Mary, Jesus' mother, being made to watch him die upon the cross.

Life isn't going to be pain-free, but God is always there for us to lean on. Every moment you are going through a hardship, He is there with you to hold you and equip you to get through. In the end, the glory He reveals to us will have made all our suffering worth it.

I consider that our present sufferings
are not worth comparing
with the glory
that will be revealed in us.
—Romans 8:18

More Proof of God's Love

Riches take wings,
comforts vanish, hope withers away,
but love stays with us. Love is God.
—Lew Wallace
Author of Ben Hur
A Tale of Christ

You're not alone in thinking God has left you during a time of strife. In Psalm 23 David even struggled to feel God's love. No one seems to know why he wrote this Psalm. Was it at the time his son died? Or could it be around the time he realized someone knew he sent a man to his death? Let's look over this Psalm and see how it could have given David peace during a time of strife.

Psalm 23

"The Lord is my shepherd, I lack nothing.
He makes me lie down in green pastures,
he leads me beside quiet waters,
he refreshes my soul.
He guides me along the right paths
for his name's sake.
Even though I walk
through the darkest valley,
I will fear no evil,
for you are with me;
your rod and your staff,
they comfort me.
You prepare a table before me
in the presence of my enemies.
You anoint my head with oil;
my cup overflows.
Surely your goodness and love will follow me
all the days of my life,
and I will dwell in the house of the Lord
forever."

In the beginning, using the words, "The Lord is my Shepherd," David is comparing God to a shepherd who tends his flock. A shepherd takes care of his sheep, feeding them, and protecting them.

Then there's the line "he leads me beside quiet waters." Some scholars believe this represents peace and harmony. Move on to "he refreshes my soul." Could that be the tranquility you feel when God repairs a broken heart?

"Your rod and your staff, they comfort me" is directly related to the comparison of God as shepherd. A rod and staff not only guide a shepherd's flock, but it protects them from wild animals as well. God will protect us from the evil one.

Though there is enough here for a short Bible study within itself, let's skip down to "You anoint my head with oil." When someone was anointed with oil in Biblical times, it was a sign of dignity.

Next go to "my cup overflows." This means that you have more than you need. Not only are your needs met, but in some instances so are your wants.

This Psalm is so full of proof of God's love, yet so many people miss it because of the "shadow of death" part. We become scared, thinking about dying. But we need to read each line to get the essence of how much God loves us. And even in our dark times, He is there for us.

And though this compares God to a shepherd, some of the lines show us proof of God as a loving father. He protects. He guides. He loves. You can't ask for a lot more than that out of either a loving god or loving father.

The love which moves the world,
according to common Christian belief,
is God's love and the love of God
—Mortimer Adler
Philospher and Author[xxvii]

Prayer

Below is a prayer to help you when those childhood feelings of abandonment pop up. I hope you find it useful.

My Father,

While I know you are a loving god, I have trouble understanding why you allow your children to suffer. Please forgive me for my lack of trust at times like those. Hold on to me when I feel alone and abandoned. Let me know you have always been there with me. I don't need to understand why you allow me to feel pain, but help me realize there is a reason for it in the end. Please, continue to shower your love upon me, Lord.
In Jesus' name,
Amen

To Dig Deeper

A: Here are some questions to help you dig a bit deeper into your relationship with God.

1. What is the one thing that keeps you from trusting in God to the fullest?

2. When was the last time you had a terrible experience like a cancer scare or a loved one ill? Who did you turn to first? Why?

3. Sometimes we find ourselves in a situation where we've felt like we didn't belong. Maybe a party at a spouse's work or a wedding where you were not familiar with either bride or groom. Think back to the last time you felt that uncomfortable feeling. How did you get through the situation?

4. Have you ever doubted God's love for you? It's only natural

to question events in our lives, so don't feel bad admitting it. Did you ever tell anyone? Why? Would you be comfortable sharing those doubts now?

5. In the second section of this chapter, I created a list of how I sometimes view myself and Bible verses that show how God sees me. I titled it My Views/God's Views. If you have not done so, do one for yourself now. Once done, add a third column titled Emotion knowing God's opinion. It should look something like:

My View ~ God's View ~ Emotion knowing God's Opinion

6. We deciphered some of Psalm 23. Are there any other lines that particularly touch you? How and why?

B: Read the following Bible verses and answer the questions to discover further proof of God's love.

1. Psalm 91:1-2: "Whoever dwells in the shelter of the Most High will rest in the shadow of the Almighty. I will say of the Lord, "He is my refuge and my fortress, my God, in whom I trust."

a. What are you needing rest from today? Have you given your problem to Jesus yet? If not, pray about it now.

b. What picture comes to mine when you think of a fortress? How about when you think of refuge?

2. I love imagery and so many verses give us such great ways to imagine God. Zephaniah 3:17, "The Lord your God is with you, the Mighty Warrior who saves. He will take great delight in you; in his love he will no longer rebuke you, but will rejoice over you with singing."

a. Close your eyes and picture God singing to you. What type of feelings does it evoke?

b. Described as the "mighty warrior," what type of armor do you picture God wearing?

3. We should not only go to God with our problems, but we are to praise Him during our time of suffering. Philippians 4:6-7, "Do not be anxious about anything, but in everything by prayer and supplication with thanksgiving let your requests be made known to God. And the peace of God, which surpasses all understanding, will guard your hearts and your minds in Christ Jesus."

a. Even though we might go to God in times of need, why is it hard for us to praise Him when we've got a problem?

b. What type of reaction do you get when you hear the words "peace of God" and that He will "guard your heart and your mind?"

4. God is a constant. He is the same today and tomorrow, just like He was yesterday. Hebrews 13:8, "Jesus Christ is the same yesterday and today and forever."

a. The world is changing every day, not always for the better. Come up with three words to describe how you feel knowing God is always the same.

b. Some people in my church will back into a parking spot so they can get out faster when service is over. Why do you think it is we seem to be in a hurry to leave God's presence?

c. People will also wait in line for days to get the latest, yet we don't seem so willing to on Sunday mornings, wanting the service over so we don't miss the football game. How often do you put things before God? Why do you think we are more willing to put God second, sometimes even third or fourth in our lives?

CHAPTER THREE
The Emotions
That Take Over Our Lives

Forgiving is rediscovering
the shining path of peace
that at first you thought others took away
when they betrayed you.
—*Dodinsky,*
author of
In the Garden of Thoughts[xxviii]

———————

Remember playing ball as a kid? Some children are good at sports, others not so much. I was one of the "not so much," and was usually chosen last. Being overweight and not athletic, no one wanted me on their team.

It's like that with my writing some days. At times, I feel I'm sitting in the slush pile. That's a term used in publishing where authors send in a letter basically saying, "pick my book." These query letters go into a pile with others, and we have to wait for someone to read and respond, hoping it's not a typical "thanks, but no thanks," form letter.

Imagine if God had a slush pile. How many of you think you'd make it to the top? Unfortunately, too many of us don't think we stand out, so we see ourselves as buried in a pile with a lot of others ahead of us. We compare ourselves to those we feel are better. We don't see any attributes to offer in order to be chosen as a favorite.

We feel unimportant to God and everyone else.

A father's attention can help his daughter with these emotions. It makes me happy to see my son-in-law take my granddaughter on father/daughter dates and out fishing with him. He makes a point of letting her know she matters.

Unfortunately, my father never made me feel that way, so I turned to alcohol. Drinking seemed to bury those feelings. I was no longer awkward when I drank. People seemed to want to be around me. Of course, most of that was because I had the only car, so I drove us to the bars.

If I look back, I realize I was probably never that important to most of the people I hung with. I was just the person who got them to the party.

Dad rejects, so others do too. At least that's how I saw it. I still do at times.

There were those in the Bible who didn't feel they measured up either. Did you know Moses didn't want the job of saving God's people? He made excuses to try to change God's mind. In Exodus 4:10, Moses says to God, 'Pardon your servant, Lord. I have never been eloquent, neither in the past nor since you have spoken to your servant. I am slow of speech and tongue.'"

I'll bet you never thought of Moses as having anything bad to say about himself, did you? His words are a sign of self-hate and insecurity. We all have these doubts in our abilities to some point. Some just hold them deeper and longer than others.

———

It's time to free ourselves
of past hurts.
To move forward
into a life of love and happiness.

———

God wants you to know you are important. You have your own

unique qualities that can be used to help others. It's hard for some of us to see this because of past hurts. We allow our past to hold us in place like superglue.

All these emotions that keep us from moving forward are basically spiritual warfare from the devil. He wants to keep our attention on the past so we can't enjoy the future. Those thoughts of unworthiness tend to hold us hostage with bitterness, regret, guilt, shame, and self-pity.

The worst part is we don't want to admit we have these feelings. If so, then we have to deal with them. Facing a past filled with pain can cause even more pain. But you have to realize that the past can only hurt us if we allow it. The more we face these issues, the less likely we are to allow them to control our lives.

And nothing can cause pain more than the loneliness of bitterness or the paranoia that guilt and shame bring in.

It's time to free ourselves of past hurts. If we can figure out why we hurt and be willing to give it away, we can move forward into a life of love and happiness. And while we might think we want to be free of our pain, some of us hold on with a tight-fisted grip because we've had these emotions too long to live without them.

You can rid yourself of these emotions that hold you down. Just reach up and allow God's hand to pull you from the slush pile. It's not always easy, but in time, you will get better at taking hold of God when times are tough or when the past invades.

You gain strength,
courage and confidence
by every experience
in which you really stop
to look fear in the face.
You are able to say to yourself,
"I have lived through this horror
I can take the next thing
that comes along."
—Eleanor Roosevelt,
Former First Lady
of the United States[xxixx]

Will I Ever Be Worthy

GOD is in the hearts of all,
and they that seek
shall surely find Him
when they need Him most.
*—Louisa May Alcott,
author of Little Women*[xxx]

———————

Finally, that man you've been eyeing in church has asked you out. Your hair looks great. That new dress fits just right. Then you hear it. A voice in your head that says, "Why would he want someone like you?" All your negative memories come crashing in around you, taking your self-confidence and ruining your evening.

Memories, especially bad ones, have a tendency to invade our minds at the most inopportune time. We think we're over our pasts, then these visions pop into our heads. Ugly emotions crash through when we're at our happiest. They can also occur at the same time each year during holidays, anniversaries, or birthdays.

My darkest emotions seem to occur around Father's Day. Not because fathers don't deserve a holiday as much as Mom, but because ads depicting great fathers are all over the place. And then I get to sit through a sermon about wonderful fathers. Eventually, anger rears its ugly head. Each June, I feel a sense of loss from the nonexistent relationship I had with my father. The sad part is he died a few years ago so I'll never have a chance at the relationship I wanted. Worse is the guilt. There is no sense of loss because he's gone physically, only for what might have been. The same loss I've felt for years when he was alive.

I doubt I'm alone with these types of feelings. A lot of women rewind the old reel in their heads and wonder why. We don't let go because we make that "why" into a word with capital letters instead of lower case. Eventually looking back dominates our world. We use our past to justify our current actions or situation and limit our future.

Why do we hold on to the past that causes us pain? One reason is protection. We believe that if we focus on what hurt us before, we won't be hurt the same way again.

You are a wonderful person.
You are a king's daughter.
And God really does love you.

By holding on to the quicksand that is our past, we can't move forward into the life God wants us to enjoy. Things like anger, bitterness, and self-pity have a way of blogging us down. We need to get rid of these emotions that continue to hold us hostage.

But how do you leave bad memories in the past where they belong?

The same way you eat an elephant. A bite at a time. Only with your past, it's a step at a time. It's not going to be easy or quick, but in time you should be able to put your past where it belongs. Behind you.

So easy to say, not so easy to do.

With God's help, you can work through anything.

Realize we have a habit of distorting our past as well. Was Dad really that bad? Am I exaggerating as to how he treated me? In some instances, we romanticize the pain to get attention or to justify why our life is a mess. It's easier to blame a bad childhood than to look in a mirror.

By moving forward and focusing on the present, you can put behind the ugly emotions that zap your day. This will give you strength to focus on the following truths: You are a wonderful person. You are a king's daughter. And God really does love you.

As you walk with Jesus,
resting your head on His heart,
you will learn to know His Word,
His will, and His ways.
You will want to obey Him,
not out of forced compliance,
but out of heartfelt connection.
Your joy will abound
as you remain in His love.
—Sue Detweiler,
author of
9 Traits of a
Life-Giving Mom[xxxi]

The Sour Taste Won't Go Away

It is a simple
but sometimes forgotten truth
that the greatest enemy
to present joy and high hopes
is the cultivation of retrospective bitterness.
—Sir Robert Menzies,
Prime Minister of Australia[xxxii]

Society has created generations of throwaway kids. Parents these days seem to put themselves first, leaving the kids to "deal with it." Unfortunately, these same parents don't give their children the knowhow to "deal with it," so they turn to drugs and gangs in order to fill a void from their parents' absence. And fathers are gone far more than mothers.

Instead, mothers flit from relationship to relationship creating pretend families in the hopes of filling a hole they themselves have inside. A hole most probably crated by not having a healthy relationship with their own father.

A father's absence, whether physically or emotionally, can affect his daughter's future relationships with men. These women find it hard to form strong bonds with any man for fear of being abandoned again. They go from man to man hoping to fill the pain created by their father's emotional distance. Without realization, this type of behavior is then passed down to their daughters.

A father who was there physically, but who might have been mentally absent, can raise a daughter who spends a lifetime picking the wrong partner. She'll choose men unworthy of her love just to keep from being alone. These same men come and go in her life, only caring about their needs, not hers.

In time hatred forms and anger sets in. The world has kicked her in the teeth so many times, she can't count. She has every right to her anger, but in the end, she can't let go. All she sees are past hurts. There's no way to enjoy the present with all the pain she holds on to from the past.

Women hang on to their pasts likes Ebenezer Scrooge held on to money. We replay incidents trying to figure ways to change what occurred, wishing we'd done something different. We don't seem to realize that we can't infuse love into a relationship with someone who wasn't around or didn't know how to love in return.

Unfortunately, the more we revisit these past hurts, the more it can lead to bitterness about what might have been. Dr. Judith Sills puts it this way, "… there's a point where appreciation and analysis of the past become gum on your psychological shoe. It sticks you in place, impedes forward motion, and like gum, it doesn't just disappear on its own. You need to do some scraping."

We rehash over and over how people have hurt us and get stuck to the past.

We trap ourselves into wanting a rewind. In the backs of our mind voices constantly tell us we did wrong. Even if it was our father who left or hurt us physically, emotionally, or sexually, we always end up wanting to go back in the hopes we can fix the relationship or say something to change the outcome.

A father should be a role model for his daughter. Yet, women who weren't raised with a good father-figure might end up more aggressive and develop unhealthy relationships with others. They see themselves as failures when in reality it was their father who was the failure. These women make poor decisions that begin in childhood and continue into adulthood.

No matter how many times we hear that there's no going back, we still beat ourselves up with "coulda beens", "should've beens", or "what ifs." And in the end, we allow bitterness to invade our lives.

Bitterness is like trying to rewrite a book we weren't the author of. Instead of getting to the end and closing the cover, we reopen and reread all the parts that hurt us in the hopes we can change things. In most instances, the person you're angry with has no idea or doesn't care. They go on with their lives as if nothing has ever happened. Yet you stay firmly planted, unable to let go.

If we give bitterness an inch of our lives, it will blister into a scab that gets picked off every once in while just so we can watch it bleed.

Every day women are held in bondage by bitterness because of what has been done to them. We no longer look for the light that could free us because we're convinced there's nothing that can be done to make us forget.

The devil thrives on bitterness. He likes to cause anger and resentment, jealousy, envy, hatred and revengeful thoughts. All ingredients for preparing his favorite stew. Like a pot of boiling water on a hot stove, bitterness simmers first, then boils, and, if not dealt with, will explode onto everything and everyone in its path.

———

If the person who hurt you
is truly evil,
nothing will irritate them more
than to see you happy.

———

Painful events of our past can tangle us into a vine that consumes us. We blame someone else for our source of unhappiness. Yet, if we were to let go, we'd receive the peace we desire.

Don't think bitterness is just for non-Christians either. Look around your church.

There is always that one woman who looks like she ate sour lemons before arriving for Sunday service. She snubs most people as she marches to her particular pew, barely acknowledging anyone. If someone were to speak with her, she only seems to complain about her health or her terrible life. And God save the person who might be sitting in her spot. While she might not say anything, the daggers shot from her eyes would be enough for most people to get the hint and move over.

Bitterness is nothing new.

In Genesis 4, the story of Cain and Abel tells of what occurs when you allow bitterness to take over a relationship. Cain did what a lot of people do, he allowed jealousy to turn to hate. His brother, Abel, was doing the right thing, but all Cain could see was that God was pleased with his brother. We're told this in Genesis 4:4, "And Abel also brought an offering--fat portions from some of the firstborn of his flock. The Lord looked with favor on Abel and his offering." Cain brought an offering also, just not his best. Instead of fixing this error, he fixated on the fact God did like his offering as well as his brother's.

That jealously festered until Cain turned so bitter, he killed his brother.

This type of anger is alive and well today when one sibling believes the another is favored. That's usually how bitterness begins, with another emotion. Jealousy, anger, or resentment. It might never get acted upon to the point of harming another physically, but it's still murder in your heart. And a little of your peace disappears each time you think about it.

We must rid our minds of this evil emotion or it'll tear us up inside. Ephesians 4:31 states, "Put out of your life all these things: bad feelings about other people, anger, temper, loud talk, bad talk which hurts other people, and bad feelings which hurt other people."

Some people refuse to admit this bitterness. But there are a couple of ways to tell if you're carrying around hatred for another.

The best way is by looking at where you focus your attention. When we're bitter toward someone or something in our past, we can't focus on anything else. It becomes our idol. We keep our mind on that one particular point in time.

And the devil dances.

When we hold on to bitterness, we lose that desired close relationship with God.

Another clue that we live with a bitter heart is by reviewing our relationships. Do people come and go quickly? Bitterness causes us to live in misery. We not only destroy our own life, but the relationships around us. No one wants to be around someone who is never happy. And when we find ourselves alone, we end up blaming our past, our spouse, children, even God for our unhappiness. It's never that person in the mirror who refuses to let go of the past.

As we learned earlier, In 1 Samuel 18, King Saul allowed fear and bitterness to eat at him to the point he tried to kill David. Here was a man who was king. Saul had power and wealth. But he allowed jealousy to overshadow any good he could have done.

Women do the same thing. Our anger smolders until it turns into a full-blown fire. We don't seem to notice that bitterness is decaying us from the inside out.

If you find yourself so focused on the past that it's destroying your relationships with others, you have to rid yourself of those ill feelings.

Give it up to God.

I know. I know. Not an easy thing to do, especially if you've been carrying this anger around like your favorite purse. But it is necessary if you want to free your mind.

The following is a list of some ways to get through bitterness. Try one or all to see if any help. Freeing yourself should be a top priority or you'll never feel joy in your life.

Pick up your Bible. Reading verses that give you peace will help you work through the pain.

Write down what has you angry. What has happened that you are having a hard time releasing? Then come up with a plan of forgiveness.

Pray for the person who caused this bitterness in the first place. I've discovered it's hard to be angry at those you're praying for.

Another way to get over bitterness is by helping others. In time, you will see some of that anger dissipate. How can you think of your father and his new family when you're reading a book to a dying child? Set your attention on others who are in need. It's one of the best ways to get your focus off yourself and onto Jesus, where it belongs.

Also, pray for God to delete any bitterness from your heart. Isaiah 38:17 reads, "See, it was for my own well-being that I was bitter. But You have kept my soul from the grave that destroys. You have put all my sins behind Your back."

Talk with others. Start with God first. Walk up the path to God's door and knock. Then once inside, let Him know everything that happened and how you feel. In time, you can let all this anger go. Then contact one of your Christian sisters and ask her to pray for you as well.

Listen to Christian music. The more you surround yourself with God's word, the less the devil can penetrate your mind.

Here's a little secret you'll probably enjoy, especially if you have a revengeful streak like me. If the person who hurt you is truly evil, nothing will irritate them more than to discover you're happy. Talk about the best revenge.

Women who grew up with unloving fathers carry bitterness from one relationship to another. Eventually they turn it on God. They blame Him and can't see He would never hurt them. We allow bitterness to hold us hostage and keep us from our Father's love when what we need to do is turn to Him to get rid of that emotion.

Philippians 4:4-7 reminds us to "Rejoice in the Lord always; again I will say, rejoice! Let your gentle spirit be known to all men. The Lord is near. Be anxious for nothing, but in everything by prayer and supplication with thanksgiving let your requests be made known to God. And the peace of God, which surpasses all comprehension, will guard your hearts and your minds in Christ Jesus."

We sometimes confuse joy with happiness, but they are two different things. Joy is something deep within your heart. John 15:11 says, "I have told you this so that my joy may be in you and that your joy may be complete." Joy is a gift from God. Happiness comes when something special happens, like having a new grandchild. Joy, on the other hand, occurs when you feel God's love daily, no matter your circumstances.

Happiness is fleeting whereas joy is deeper. When we are aware of God's love in our lives, joy can be forever. But in order to obtain this happiness, we have to get rid of the bitterness that is filling our hearts.

It's not always easy to forgive someone who has hurt you. You might even be justified in the anger you hold towards another. That situation is only worsened when the person was never punished. However, if you don't forgive, you will never be free of them. They will constantly be on your mind.

Give up whatever has you tasting that bitter bill of resentment. Lay it down at Jesus' feet and turn away, leaving it behind. Matthew 11:28 says, "Come to me, all you who are weary and burdened, and I will give you rest." Only God can give you rest from the bitterness you've been carrying.

No matter how many times
we hear that there's no going back,
we still beat ourselves up with
"coulda beens",
"should've beens",
or "what ifs."

God wants you to turn over all your hurts, fears, and anger to Him, but it's not always easy. When someone has victimized you to the point of severe pain, whether physical or emotional, you want to see them pay. It's a natural human reaction. However, the best thing you can do is allow God to deal with them while you move on and heal.

Go to Him, and allow Him to help you. Pray that the tar coating your insides is replaced by God's love.

We should focus on the path before us, not on what is behind.

Living an overflowing life of God's love comes from having a personal relationship with Jesus Christ. It is being aware that you are God's daughter, and you are loved. He is the source of all joy.

Joy can only be found through grace or forgiveness that only God can give. It is also the only way to become independent from bitterness and anger. Accept God's love now. Feel the freedom from bitterness and take what is rightfully yours as God's daughter.

When you hold onto a script
that doesn't serve you,
you leave no space
to write a new one that does.
—Jennifer Ho-Dougatz,
Owner of United Tribe[xxxiv]

If I Could Only Go Back

Live your life without the regrets,
without the resentments,
without the unforgiveness,
without the blame game,
without the self-pity,
without any and everything
that keeps you from
experiencing true joy within!
You are too important
to waste your life away!
Learn to appreciate and value your life,
but most importantly,
learn to appreciate and value yourself!
You count too,
no matter what you've done!
—Stephanie Lahart,
author of
Teens Matter Most[xxxv]

Have you ever dreamed of going back in time? All of us do. It's been the basis of countless books, movies, and even television shows like Quantum Leap. If you could go back, what would you change in the course of history? What about in your own past?

There isn't one of us who doesn't wish we could change something in our past. Times when we've hurt others, spent money instead of saved, fell in love too quickly, etc. We all live with regrets. If I'd only purchased Microsoft stock when it first went on sale, I'd be set for life. If I'd never bought that five-bedroom house I couldn't afford, then I wouldn't be so far in debt. If I'd only married my high school sweetheart, things would be so much better.

Then there's the regrets about what others have done to us. A big one for daughters with bad relationships with their fathers is If only Dad had loved me. Inevitably women who feel abandoned by their fathers, grow to regret his actions as much as their own. Even though there was nothing they could do about how he treated her.

Fathers don't realize that what they say doesn't mean as much as what they do. Actions speak so much louder than words. Tell your daughter you'll be there to pick her up for the weekend then don't show up. You've shown her she isn't important. And then she begins to wonder what's wrong with her that her own father doesn't want her.

I recall coming home one day with all A's and B's on my report card. This was the first time I'd done so well. Usually I was a C student. I was so proud. My sister and brother each had their usual, my sister was like me, an average student, my brother near the bottom. However, my dad didn't say much to them, but when he saw mine, he said, "You can do better." Maybe he was trying to encourage me, but all I heard was You'll never be good enough.

I never did that well in school again until college. I basically saw myself as a failure. To this day, I still carry those feelings of inadequacy.

When a book doesn't sell well, I hear You'll never make it as an author. Give up. Stop wasting your time. It doesn't matter how many awards I've received, I still feel like a loser. All because words from my past set a tone for how I see myself today.

How many of you out there berate yourself the same way?

Well, let me tell you something ladies, there's nothing wrong with us. (One day I hope to believe it.) The issue was your father's, so don't carry his garbage on your back, According to Edward Kruk, Ph.D, these issues of insecurities and "other social problems correlate more strongly with fatherlessness than with any other factor, surpassing race, social class and poverty, father absence may well be the most critical social issue of our time."

After years of regret, you're probably wondering how you get rid of something you've clinged to for so long. As a start, let's look at that word regret. According to Dictionary.com, regret is defined as "a sense of loss, dissatisfaction, or disappointment."

Disappointment is the least of our hang-ups. This regret issue ultimately eats us up on the inside. It hits women right in the middle of their foreheads.

We all live with regret, but women seem to hold onto it more than men. And a lot of that anguish comes from how others have treated us. We look back and wonder what we could have done differently. Women with abusive or neglectful fathers are the worst for beating themselves up because they never learned to deal with the "what ifs" that life hands us. They continually say mean things to themselves. If only I'd gotten better grades, maybe Dad would have stayed. If only I'd told Mom what he did to me, maybe he wouldn't have hurt someone else.

If only… If only… If only…

After a while, we start to believe those inner thoughts are coming from God. We turn our regret into self-hate, when in most cases our fathers just weren't good fathers.

No matter what you've gone through,
God has a plan.

Regret nags at our subconscious, continually reminding us of our past.

People in the Bible were probably no different. I imagine Adam and Eve wished they hadn't spoken to the serpent. Talk about regret. They ended up not only getting tossed out of Heaven, but one son killed the other. I'm sure David regretted the way King Saul treated him, wondering what he could have done differently to keep the man from hating to the point of murder. Jesus probably also regretted that He hadn't saved his cousin John the Baptist from being beheaded.

Regret is something we live with each day. Things like wishing we'd left five minutes earlier so we wouldn't be stuck in traffic are small regrets that eat up our happiness.

When it comes to past hurts, our Godly Father is more than able to squelch the pain. All too often we forget that all it takes is asking Him to help us and He does. And remember, no matter what you've gone through, God has a plan for why.

Think about the story of Esther. I'm sure she regretted getting being taken by the king, but God used it for good. Her uncle explained to her in Esther 4:14, "' For if you remain silent at this time, relief and deliverance for the Jews will arise from another place, but you and your father's family will perish. And who knows but that you have come to your royal position for such a time as this?'" God used her position as queen to save His people.

Esther had been put in a terrible situation, but God turned it for the good. And He will do the same for you if you allow him the chance.

In Isaiah 43:18-19, the bible tells us "Do not remember the things that have happened before. Do not think about the things of the past. See, I will do a new thing. It will begin happening now. Will you not know about it? I will even make a road in the wilderness, and rivers in the desert." By letting go of the past, we can receive a new beginning, one where our knowledge in Jesus who will allow us less regrets in the future.

Sometimes we can be our harshest critic, but our loving Father will be there to help us and show us we are worthy of being the King's daughter.

Follow God's example. If He can forgive your past discretions, whether real or perceived, through our fault or no fault of our own, who are we to hold it against ourselves? Are we better than God? No. So, forgive yourself the way He has already forgiven you.

We are hard on ourselves,
quick to point an accusatory finger inward,
and prone to believe our condemning thoughts
are directed by God himself.
—Christine Hoover, Author[xxxvii]

The Black Hole in My Heart

Trauma is personal.
It does not disappear
if it is not validated.
When it is ignored or invalidated
the silent screams continue internally
heard only by the one held captive.
When someone enters the pain
and hears the screams
healing can begin.
—Danielle Bernock,
author of Emerging With Wings:
A True Story of Lies, Pain,
and the Love that Heals[xxxviii]

What is the worst thing you've ever done in your life? Something so devastating you can't let go? An affair? Stealing? An abortion?

Chances are, whatever it is, you haven't told many people. That secret hides in the blackest place in your heart in a room called Shame. Shame lives where no one else can feel it but you. It likes to hang out with guilt.

Both have a tendency to lurk around only to come out at times when we should be our happiest. That voice announces, "Remember when" loud and clear. There's also "You aren't deserving." It's a flash in the middle of your day that says, "I'm no good."

These words crash around us like a building being demolished. We implode hoping no one can see.

A loving father can relieve some of the guilt his daughter carries just by saying "It's not your fault" or "You're forgiven." Unfortunately, too many fathers or father-figures are responsible for this guilt through acts of molestation and sexual abuse.

Guilt and shame go hand-in-hand, but are also very different. Guilt makes a person feel bad for something they've done whereas shame tells them they're bad. Guilt goes after the action, shame attacks the person. Guilt will say "I can't believe you just hurt her." Shame yells, "You are worthless because of what you've done."

However, when it comes to something as awful as molestation or sexual abuse, it's worse. The words become "How could you let him do that?" or "Why didn't you tell? You must have wanted it." Shame crawls over us like a coating of paint that can't be washed away with the strongest turpentine.

The evil one uses guilt and shame to destroy us. By dwelling in the world of guilt and shame, we spend our time looking inward. Shame causes women to develop unhealthy habits such as alcoholism, drug use, even obesity. . We use any form of self-harm in the hopes no one finds out why we're hurting.

At times shame can also show on a person's body with such things as stooped shoulders, dark circles from lack of sleep, extreme weight gain, or weight loss. We take out the actions of our pasts on ourselves, both mentally and physically.

Hateful whispers fill us. We berate ourselves in our own minds constantly. We tell ourselves that God can't love someone like me because of what happened. That voice in our head keeps reminding us that "once a sinner, always a sinner." Guilt and shame can hold a woman hostage better than any international terrorist.

To make matters worse, paranoia gets added to mix when shame says, "Wait until other people find out."

By keeping our secrets, we help shame to grow. Shame likes to live in silence. The last thing it wants is for you to shine a light on what happened. However, by sharing your story, you can not only free yourself, but help others who have gone through the same thing.

Everyone has lived with shame and guilt to some degree. Cheating on a test, lying to their parents, stealing. Even the disciples were caught up in the guilt and shame game.

————————

To some, women are seen as vulnerable,
yet by exposing our emotions and past hurts,
we actually show true courage.

————————

In Luke 22:56-60, Peter denied Jesus three times. "Then a servant girl, seeing him as he sat in the light and looking closely at him, said, 'This man also was with him [Jesus].' But he denied it, saying, 'Woman, I do not know him.' And a little later someone else saw him and said, 'You also are one of them.' But Peter said, 'Man, I am not.' And after an interval of about an hour still another insisted, saying, 'Certainly this man also was with him, for he too is a Galilean.' But Peter said, 'Man, I do not know what you are talking about.'"

Even after all the miracles and time Peter had spent with the Lord, fear caused him to deny He knew Jesus. I imagine he lived with a good deal of guilt and shame once Jesus was put to death. In fact, after he denied Jesus, in Luke 22:61-62, it reads, And the Lord turned and looked at Peter. And Peter remembered the saying of the Lord, how he had said to him, "Before the rooster crows today, you will deny me three times." And he went out and wept bitterly."

Peter wept because he let his friend and savior down. His fear turned to guilt and shame when he realized an earlier prediction of Jesus' came true.

David also lived with guilt after his affair with Bathsheba. How can I tell he felt guilty? Because you don't try to fix or hide things if you did nothing wrong.

Once Bathsheba became pregnant, he tried to fix his sin by bringing her husband, Uriah, home from the war in order to have sex with her. However, out of respect for his fellow soldiers, Uriah refused to sleep with her. David then moved on to plan B. He had

Uriah taken to the front lines to fight, knowing he would be killed. David not only had to live with the guilt of an affair, but now the shame of murder as well.

Some biblical scholars believe Psalm 32 is proof of David's grief over his shame. Psalm 32 reads in part, "When I kept silent about my sin, my body wasted away through my groaning all day long. For day and night Your hand was heavy upon me; My vitality was drained away as with the fever heat of summer."

I'm going to tell you a secret not many people know, but my grandfather molested me when I was a preteen. It took years for me to tell someone only to discover he had done the same thing to her. I lived with a lot of guilt because if I'd said something, maybe she wouldn't have been hurt. But, I always thought it was my fault or that I really wanted the attention.

Isn't that what happens to sexual assault victims. Others accuse them of being at fault. Every time my grandfather finished, he'd give me a bite-sized piece of chocolate. I was a fat kid. Who knows, maybe I allowed it for the candy.

Guilt is a terrible thing for a child to live with.

Everyone has something in their past they want to keep secret. But I'll almost guarantee someone you know has gone through the same thing you have.

That's why God put you in their way, to help them by being able to say, "I've been there, too." That could be why God had me write this book, to help others who have felt abandoned and unloved for years.

To some, women are seen as vulnerable, yet by exposing our emotions and past hurts, we actually show true courage. Sure, we have breakdowns, crying jags, and downright hissy fits (or maybe that's just me), but when we share our problems with others, and show our vulnerability, we all grow.

Susceptibility comes during a time when shame attacks. Having the courage to get help from God or other Godly women moves you closer to healing. It helps deepen your connection with your Father.

God didn't create us to suffer alone. That's why He gave us sisters. Those we can talk to and lean on. Galatians 6:2 says we are to "Bear one another's burdens, and so fulfill the law of Christ." Telling a trusted friend about what is bothering you can give you relief.

The devil likes to convince us we'll never be any good after what happened. The more we believe him, the less we're listening to the word of God. However, our Father's voice can drown out Satan and the pain of shame. We just need to open our hearts to Him.

One of Satan's favorite lines is, "You're not worth it." That's a lie he uses to keep us down. But what happened to you is not who you are. You are no longer an alcoholic, and you are not unloved.

I am no longer a victim of molestation. I am a daughter of a King. And no matter what you went through, so are you.

We need to stop listening to the lies of the devil. Instead, listen to God when He says He loves you. Then hear these words of our savior, "I died for you, and you are worth it."

———

God will not look you over
for medals,
degrees or diplomas
but for scars.
—*Elbert Hubbard,*
Writer and Artist[xl]

———

Let the Pity-Party Begin

Come to me,
all who labor and are heavy laden,
and I will give you rest.
Take my yoke upon you,
and learn from me,
for I am gentle and lowly in heart,
and you will find rest for your souls.
For my yoke is easy,
and my burden is light.
—Matthew 11:28-30

Suicide, crime, and discord are running rampant in this world. People are looking for something to believe in. We all want to feel peace and love - it just doesn't always happen, no matter how good our life might be going. At times, there are going to be empty spaces.

How many of us live in a never-ending barrage of unhappiness because of our past hurts? We become so focused on a childhood of unlove that we end up living in the land of self-pity. It's like we can't get enough of the "poor me" syndrome. Some of us bask in it. Self-pity becomes so comfortable; it's like a warm, cozy fire. No matter the situation, people who live with self-pity have to find a way to bring the conversation back to their woe-is-me life.

I know someone like this. No one is ever as sick as she is. No one is ever as overworked either. No matter what happens in her life, it's always someone else's fault.

Self-pity can be a debilitating attribute. At times it comes out of fear. It's been known to hold people in addiction. "I wouldn't drink if it weren't for . . . ." Spiritual teacher Deepak Chopra states that self-pity "arises because you feel no one will lift you out of your difficulties."

No one else can make you happy. You need to be dependent on Jesus for your joy.

Not easy.

Women who grew up feeling abandoned or betrayed don't have the knowhow to move forward. How do you like yourself when your own father didn't? And the more we look inward, the more we intensify these feelings of self-hate, making it hard to move to a life of joy.

In the Bible story of Ruth, she could have played the self-pity game. In Biblical times, it was common for women to live with their husband's family. If something happened to their husband, other men in the family were to take care of them. But by the time Naomi's husband died, so had her brother-in-law, and father-in-law. That left three women with no one to care for them in a time when women couldn't find a job. Instead of feeling sorry for herself and returning to her own family, Ruth stayed with her mother-in-law to help her.

She focused on someone else. She didn't look inward though she must have been scared of what the future held.

As long as you look outward instead of inward, you will move foward. I'm sure you're saying to yourself right now, "But Kathryn, you don't know what happened to me." You're right. I don't. But I do know you need to get out of the self-pity pit before it destroys you permanently.

There are a few simple steps you can take to pull you out of the hole of self-pity. Try one or all to have yourself standing on firm ground in no time.

1. One of the best ways to step off the self-pity bandwagon is to acknowledge your past. Yes, something bad happened to you. But right here, right now, I want you to make this your new slogan: "This happened to me but I made it through because I'm strong." Don't just read it, say it out loud. Now, say it like you mean it.

Are you feeling a bit better right about now? I hope so.

But you shouldn't rely
on anyone else to make you happy.
You need to be dependent on Jesus
for your joy.

---

2.   Another step is to ask God to help you. Nothing can help tone down self-pity better than God's arms wrapped around your shoulder while you discuss your problems.

3.   As I've stated before, a good way to get over your past is to volunteer. By getting involved with others, like Ruth did, you help yourself with a myriad of problems, including depression. The more you focus on others, the less you see your own pain. Collect clothing for the homeless, feed the hungry, or read to the elderly in your area. Go on a mission trip. Find some way to keep yourself so busy, you can't think of how miserable you are. Basically, you have to get out and DO. You cannot continually think about the past if you're busy helping others.

4. Beat the self-pity blues with exercise. It's hard to feel sorry for yourself when you're breathing hard and sweating. Truthfully, exercise has been proven to help your mental state. And building muscles can be a huge pick-me-up.

5.   Read a humorous book or listen to a Christian comedian. Almost anything Erma Bombeck wrote should do the trick or go to Youtube and watch Jeanne Robertson or Chonda Pierce. Both are hilarious. You can't stay in a depressed state when you're laughing. And laughter is good for you, as stated in Proverbs 17:22, "A cheerful heart is good medicine, but a crushed spirit dries up the bones."

You think Ruth had it bad, take a look at Job. If anyone had a reason to wallow in self-pity, it was him. He lost everything. His wife, children, money, and his home. Yet he never turned away from God. Even when his friends were putting doubts in his mind, Job stayed truthful. Job 1:20-22 tells us, "...Job arose, tore his robe, and shaved his head; and he fell to the ground and worshiped. And he said, 'Naked I came from my mother's womb, And naked shall I return there. The Lord gave, and the Lord has taken away; Blessed be the name of the Lord." Throughout every tragedy, Job did not sin nor charge God with wrong. Because of this, God blessed Job even more than before.

Anytime the self-pity wagon pulls up in front of your house, read the story of Job. Trust me, in most cases, it'll make what you're going through feel like a walk in the park. If we could live with the faith of Job or Ruth, self-pity would never have power over us.

We need to toss out those streamers and noise makers we pull out every time a bad memory pops into our head. The more we live in a woe-is-me world, the less we see the light of Jesus.

Others don't want to be around someone who constantly relives their past and can never appreciate that the glass is half-full, even some of the time.

As God's daughter, you deserve nothing but His best. So, grab hold of the reigns and stop those horses pulling your self-pity wagon. Give Jesus your full attention. Any time you find yourself falling into the "woe-is-me" hole, open your Bible. The words of your Father will do more to help release you than any bar of chocolate.

Of course, combining reading of the word with chocolate might help you twice as much.

———

Self-pity in its early stage
is as snug as a feather mattress.
Only when it hardens
does it become uncomfortable.
—*Maya Angelou*[xliv]

———

Letting Go to Move Forward

We all do things
we desperately wish we could undo.
Those regrets just become
part of who we are,
along with everything else.
To spend time trying to change that,
well, it's like chasing clouds.
—*Libba Bray,*
Young Adult Novelist[xlv]

———————

Have you ever watched a running back during a football game as he's racing for the end zone? Other plays try to knock the ball from his arms, but if he holds fast, they can't pry it loose. If he fumbles, it's usually because they're more focused on scoring a goal and forget about the ball.

Women can be like that. Only our focus is on the past to the point we forget the present. We find certain events impossible to forget. Guilt, shame, and regret zap our strength and hold us glued in one place. It's the devil's way of keeping us from being happy. John 10:10 warns us in part, "The thief comes only to steal and kill and destroy."

Satan will use anything to keep us from God's joy. Any negative emotion the evil one can fling to keep us down, he will. If the devil can fully destroy your relationship with God, he'll be dancing in the street.

A loving father likes it when you turn to him in your time of distress. He likes to hear that you need Him. God is no different. He is saddened when we just walk away. Isaiah 49:15-16 says, "Can a mother forget the baby at her breast and have no compassion on the child she has borne? Though she may forget, I will not forget you! See, I have engraved you on the palms of my hands; your walls are ever before me."

Do you have your children engraved on your palms?

It's funny how women will forgive others before themselves. It's common for us to view our sins or sins against us in a harsher light. But any daughter of the King must learn to let go in order to free herself from that bondage.

The more we look behind, the more we miss out on the joy right in front of us. We have to let go in order to move forward.

Again, not easy. Try the following exercise to see if it helps.

Close your eyes and picture yourself holding a basket filled with anything painful that occurred in your past. It's a heavy basket and takes two hands to carry. You might even have to drag it in order to move it. Now, picture Jesus sitting on a beautiful throne up ahead. He motions for you to come forward. Explain to Him that you'd like to leave all your past hurts with Him so you can be happy. He nods agreement. Place the basket at His feet. Walk away. Do not look back. Take off at a run and go over two mountains. Now stop and rest.

Imagine all that weight lifted from your shoulders. Are you standing more upright? Do you feel a sense of relief or loss?

———

A loving father likes it
when you turn to him in your time of distress.
He likes to hear that you need him.
God is no different.

———

I wouldn't be surprised if you said loss. That's what most women experience in the beginning. We get used to these emotions and when we leave them behind, we feel like we're naked in public. Not only do we look back, but we want to return to Jesus, pick up our full basket, and cling to it like a favorite toy.

Change isn't easy, but with Christ's help, you can do it.

Every day repeat the exercise above, and each time go further than the last. Put more mountains between you and your basket of guilt and regret. Eventually you'll be too far away to see it once you turn around. Also, hopefully, too tired mentally to go back to retrieve it.

Later, when you start to recall what has been holding you back, and you will, ask Jesus to take your basket again.

There are other things you can do to help draw closer to God. In addition to reading the Bible daily, focus on certain verses. Also, write down anything that upsets you. Then go to the Bible and find a verse dealing with the issue.

Here are some examples.

Anger

James 1:19-20 which says, "This you know, my beloved brethren. But everyone must be quick to hear, slow to speak and slow to anger; for the anger of man does not achieve the righteousness of God."

Scared

John 14:27 which reminds us, "Peace I leave with you; my peace I give you. I do not give to you as the world gives. Do not let your hearts be troubled and do not be afraid."

Lonely

Joshua 1:9: "Have I not commanded you? Be strong and courageous. Do not be frightened, and do not be dismayed, for the LORD your God is with you wherever you go."

A good concordance can help with this. The more you go to God's word, the more you will come to rely on Him instead of your emotions.

The Bible is proof God loves you unconditionally. Verses are a wonderful way to help you move forward. Write down scriptures that speak to you. Tape them in places you are more likely to see them. The bathroom mirror, the computer screen, the television. Repeat your verses until they are ingrained in you as much as the need to breathe. Make the verses something you consistently have in your mind to the point they pop up any time your past hurts start to invade.

Allow God to free you from the grudge you've been holding toward yourself. It's time to throw your shoulders back and look up toward your Heavenly Father.

Nothing is greater. No one is more merciful, more willing to help you let go of the pain, or more loving.

———————

The truth is,
you've already been forgiven.
The truth is,
your mistakes do not define you.
The truth is,
you are not alone.
The truth is,
the grace and forgiveness of God
are bigger than all of us
and our mistakes combined.
—Sarah Markley[xlvi]

———————

More Proof of God's Love

God does not want us to live in the past. He wants us to be like the flowers in the ground that flourish. Break through your past hurts and grow into the beautiful flower He wants you to be. The following verse is from Psalm 32 that was mentioned earlier.

Psalm 32

Blessed is the one
whose transgressions are forgiven,
whose sins are covered.
Blessed is the one
whose sin the LORD does not count against them
and in whose spirit is no deceit.
When I kept silent,
my bones wasted away
through my groaning all day long.
For day and night
your hand was heavy on me;
my strength was sapped
as in the heat of summer.
Then I acknowledged my sin to you
and did not cover up my iniquity.
I said, "I will confess
my transgressions to the LORD."
And you forgave
the guilt of my sin.
Therefore let all the faithful pray to you
while you may be found;
surely the rising of the mighty waters
will not reach them.
You are my hiding place;

you will protect me from trouble
and surround me with songs of deliverance.
I will instruct you and teach you in the way you should go;
I will counsel you with my loving eye on you.
Do not be like the horse or the mule,
which have no understanding
but must be controlled by bit and bridle
or they will not come to you.
Many are the woes of the wicked,
but the LORD's unfailing love
surrounds the one who trusts in him.
Rejoice in the LORD and be glad, you righteous;
sing, all you who are upright in heart!

It is so great that God cleans our "record" of sin. It's stated that when you keep silent about sin, you waste away. Guilt can chew you up. As you can see, you are not alone when you have sin that weighs you down. David felt it too. Yet, we're also told in this Psalm that by confessing our sins, we can be relieved of our guilt. We're also reminded that God offers His unfailing love, so rejoice in His love.

Closing Prayer

Dear Father,
You are an awesome God. Thank you for being there for me during my childhood. I want nothing more than to see You as my heavenly father. Please take away my past hurts and help me focus on today and tomorrow, not yesterday. And please help me to forgive the person who hurt me, even if that person was myself. Help me to love myself the way You love me. Give me the inner peace that only You can provide. Thank you, Lord, for taking my sins and giving me the chance at everlasting joy.
In Jesus name,
Amen

To Dig Deeper:

A: Here are some questions to help you dig a bit deeper into your relationship with God.

1.   If you could change one thing in your past, what would it be? How would you vision your life today? Realize that by making just one change, your life as it is today could be different. Would you still be willing to give up that one thing if it meant losing your spouse or children?

2.   Have you shared any of your past hurts with anyone? If not, why? How about doing so now? Pray or share with a Godly friend. You might find the peace you desire.

3.   In some instances, we have a tendency to go to our friends with our problems before Jesus. Some even to social media or to do a Google search, hoping to find a solution. Why do you think that is? How do you think God sees our response to go to others first?

4.   When I mentioned earlier that there's always one person who comes to church looking like they had lemons for breakfast, who came to your mind? Have you ever prayed for this person? If not, pray for them now, and continue to pray for them until you see them next. If they appear happier, maybe a little bit of light has come into their expression due to your prayers.

5.   We've discussed several instances of the emotional impact an absent father can have on his daughter. One other thing is she can become aggressive. Think back to the girl bully in your school. She probably had a bad relationship with her father. She hurt others to make herself feel better. Knowing that today, how does it make you feel about her now? Have you ever hurt another to make yourself feel better? If so, what would you say to that person if they walked into the room right now?

B. Read the following Bible verses. Reflect on them and answer the questions that follow. How does each verse show God's love for you?

1. Psalm 103:12: "as far as the east is from the west, so far has he removed our transgressions from us."

a. We all sin and fall short of the glory of God. I have a habit with being quick to judgment. What is a habit that causes you to sin? (Gossip? Pride?) Have you asked God to help you with this issue? If not, do so now.

b. Jesus spread His arms out for us on the cross to give us a pathway to God. If you could go back and meet Jesus twenty-four hours before He was arrested and put on the cross, what one thing would you say to Him?

2. Romans 8:1-2: "Therefore, there is now no condemnation for those who are in Christ Jesus, because through Christ Jesus the law of the Spirit who gives life has set you free from the law of sin and death."

a. Jesus gave His life for us to be able to receive God's love more readily. List three to four words that describe how it feels to know Jesus died for you.

b. What does it mean to you that we now have a life free from the law of sin and death?

3. Ephesians 4:31-31, "Let all bitterness and wrath and anger and clamor and slander be put away from you, along with all malice. Be kind to one another, tenderhearted, forgiving one another, as God in Christ forgave you."

a. If you were a billionaire and could start any type of charitable organization, what would it be and why?

b. As stated a couple of times, volunteering helps with a myriad of issues. When was the last time you did any volunteer work? Have you ever taken a mission trip? If you haven't done so, is there a place you'd like to go? What's stopping you?

4. Philippians 3:13-14: "Brothers and sisters, I do not consider myself yet to have taken hold of it. But one thing I do: Forgetting what is behind and straining toward what is ahead, I press on toward the goal to win the prize for which God has called me heavenward in Christ Jesus."

a. What in this scripture helps you most when it comes to letting go of the past in order to move forward?

b. Earlier, I suggested picturing yourself putting all your painful memories in a basket and laying it Jesus' feet. What is the one memory you would love to rid yourself of today? If you didn't do the exercise, take a moment and do so now with that memory in your basket.

CHAPTER FOUR
I Want to Be Like …

The reason we struggle with insecurity
is because we compare our
behind-the-scenes
with everyone else's highlight reel.
—*Steve Furtick,*
Author and Pastor[xlvii]

"Diane, why can't you get good grades like Gloria?"
"Jenny, why don't you clean your room as well as your brother?"
Sound familiar? How many of you grew up being compared to a sibling? Why aren't you as pretty as… or as tall as… or as thin as… So many of us are insecure because we were constantly compared to others as we grew up. And it doesn't stop when we're children.

"When will you marry like your sister Sue?" "When will you have children like the rest of your friends?"

Our lives can be a never-ending barrage of comparisons. Because of this, in some cases, we think we're never good enough.

It doesn't help if our parents showed favoritism. My brother was always the favorite for one reason - he was a boy. He never did anything in the way of accomplishments, didn't even graduate high school, but Mom and Dad still favored him. My sister and I realized it from an early age.

As if that wasn't bad, then I had to go to school. My sister was a year younger, so we basically went to the same school throughout our lives. She was thin with pretty looks and curly blonde hair. I was just the opposite. A twinge of jealousy still enters in when I see a photograph of her today.

Then there are some of you who had it worse. Maybe your dad remarried, creating an entirely new family with her kids and then theirs. Your mother also remarried, leaving you to feel left out because both parents were giving all their time to their new family. You are what I call a "middling." You're in the middle of two families, but don't really belong to either anymore.

Comparing ourselves or our situations to others only leads to low self-esteem and loss of joy. You find yourself feeling bad because you don't know as much as Ellen, you don't do as many volunteer hours as April, you don't own a house like…, and the list goes on.

One of the worst habits a woman can have is comparing herself to another. Yet we do it constantly. Comparing ourselves to that starlet in the movies, former classmates, friends, our mothers, and other Christian women. And if we continually compare ourselves to other Christians, we might end up feeling inferior in our Christian walk.

When you come across a woman who knows every Bible verse off the top of her head, do feelings of inadequacy rush in? Like you're not living up to God's potential?

For me they do.

How am I supposed to compete with someone like that? There are those who can tell you the exact moment they came to Jesus. I barely recall what I had for breakfast much less where in the Bible the woman touched Jesus' cloak to stop her bleeding. I can't help but wonder if that makes them a better Christian me?

Yet, Jesus invites everyone to come as they are to the throne. Isaiah 1:18 reiterates that sentiment, "Come now, let's settle this," says the LORD. "Though your sins are like scarlet, I will make them as white as snow. Though they are red like crimson, I will make them as white as wool." This is true for everyone, not just the Billy Graham's or Mother Theresa's of the world.

Comparisons are also unfair. You don't know what that other person had to go through to get where they are. And in a lot of cases, you wouldn't want to have walked in their shoes to get where they are today.

Comparing yourself to others
is society's way of measuring people.

By comparing yourself to others, you're trying to win the approval of society instead of God's. Galatians 1:10 reads, "Am I now trying to win the approval of human beings, or of God? Or am I trying to please people? If I were still trying to please people, I would not be a servant of Christ." That is what comparisons are – people pleasing.

We compare ourselves based on what the world says we are, not on what God tells us. According to Tania Kotsos, author of the book Mind Your Reality, "Comparing yourself to others traps you in a roller-coaster ride, on which your self-worth is flung around by the opinion, words and actions of others." You never see yourself as good enough if you continually compare yourself or your situation to others.

The devil will go out of his way to reinforce those emotions. And if he can get you to compare yourself to another, you make his job easy. As long as you're focused on something you believe you're lacking, or that flaw you perceive to be there, you will never fully accept you are God's daughter.

Satan tosses out barbs like, "Look at all the time Dad spends with her because she's so cute." Or "All the other women can spout verse after verse, and you barely understand what you've just read." The evil one wants you to feel inferior.

Don't think you're alone with these mean words. Everyone gets attacked. It's how we take it that makes the difference. The devil will bully you any chance he gets. In Matthew 4:1-11, Satan even tried to bully Jesus. At Matthew 4: 2-3, it says, "After fasting forty days and forty nights, he was hungry. The tempter came to him and said, "If you are the Son of God, tell these stones to become bread."

I imagine Jesus was tired and probably weak. Along comes Satan to play his little games.

He does that with us, waits until we're at our most vulnerable to tempt us. We need to be like Jesus and not allow the devil to win. How did Jesus fight it? He tossed God's own words back at the evil one. That's why knowing the Bible is so important.

God never berates. Would a loving father tell you you're not good enough? Of course not, and God is very loving. The last thing He wants is to hurt you. God doesn't compare you with anyone else. He knows what's in your heart, and that's the most important thing. Ephesians 2:22 states, "And in him you too are being built together to become a dwelling in which God lives by his Spirit." God wants you to grow into a good Christian where His light will shine for others to see.

By listening to that voice that says you're not good enough you prove you're not listening to God. Our Father will never put you down. He's all about building up with grace, joy, and love.

Women also have a tendency to overestimate what they're seeing. It might also appear our Christian friend knows more verses of the Bible, but it could just be certain Bible stories she enjoys and reads them over and over. She may come across as well versed because of our own insecurities.

The same is true by comparing your situation to that of others, including your step or half-sibling.

Maybe your stepsister feels as left out as you do.

Instead of looking at someone else's talent, focus on your own unique gifts. You might not know Bible verses, but you could be good at reading to children. Can you turn a story into an adventure that makes kids want to listen and learn? This other woman you are comparing yourself too might fear reading out loud. God gave us each unique gifts to fulfill His plan. By comparing yourself to another, you find yourself too insecure to move forward with what God specifically has in store for you.

And realize, not all women who quote the Bible are good Christians. They're what Rick Warren, Pastor of Saddleback Church calls a "lady Clairol Christian, - nobody knows for sure, does she or doesn't she?"

Knowing scripture doesn't make one a good Christian. That just makes them knowledgeable about the Bible.

A lot of scholars also know what's in the Bible, but I don't think I'd want to follow some of their world views. Even Satan knows the Bible. Revelations 12:12 tells us to "rejoice, you heavens and you who dwell in them! But woe to the earth and the sea, because the devil has gone down to you! He is filled with fury, because he knows that his time is short." I think he's still holding out for a different ending. Boy, is he going to be disappointed.

I can't tell you where a Bible verse comes from. I can't tell you the moment I was saved. What I can tell you is God loves me anyway. He loves you as well.

You need to not measure yourself against others whether it be Christian women or half/step-siblings. The same goes with your situation or past. Maybe Dad did start a new family with someone else. Their home might have been filled with anger while yours was not. Your half-sibling might have seen your situation as the better deal.

God loves you whether you are a blond, curly haired girl or a redhead with freckles. Whether you're hips are covered with cellulite or you are muscular.

He sees each of us women through the eyes of a loving father who thinks his daughters are the most beautiful beings he created.

---

*The surest route
to breeding jealousy is to compare.
Since jealousy comes from feeling
less than another,
comparisons only fan the fires.
—Dorothy Corkill Briggs
Author of
Your Child's Self-Esteem*[1]

Waving the White Flag

Faith is the bird that feels the light
when the dawn is still dark.
—Rabindranath Tagore,
Nobel Prize Winner[li]

Do you recall the commercial years ago from Burger King? It told us we could "have it our way." It was a good advertising that sold a lot of hamburgers.

It's human nature to want to be in control. The last thing we want is for God or anyone else to have it their way. The Lord wants us to give Him full control. He wants us to accept Him as our father, and to have faith knowing that He is there when we need Him.

In order to accept all God as to offer, we must surrender our lives. Turning over the reins to someone who calls himself father, when we're not comfortable with the term, is not easy. Especially for Americans. We've been raised to fight for our country and fight for the underdog. Most of us have a "don't quit" attitude when it comes to giving in. Yet, God wants us to surrender to Him. In essence, He is asking us to wave that white flag so to speak.

Surrendering to God takes courage. I mean, if He were to ask me to go to the mission fields for five years, I'm not sure I'd be able to sell my home and go. He's been known to ask others to talk to people about Jesus in the grocery store line. For some, an overseas mission trip sounds a lot easier.

Giving up control goes against every grain in our bodies. It is scary to put all our trust in someone else, especially a being we can't see or physically touch. But if we step out of that boat like Peter did in verse Matthew 14:29, we'll realize that giving up control to God is the way to true joy.

For those who had bad father-daughter relationships, surrendering is not for the faint of heart. Those women who grew up without a loving father to guide them, women like me, make decisions based on past situations. We aren't used to asking someone else for help, especially a male figurehead.

But when we do accept God as our Heavenly Father, we also reap so much more than a loving relationship. We receive freedom from worry and inner peace like we've never known before.

The best way to build that bridge to get connected with God is by way of the Bible. Keep His word in your mind. The more you come to know Jesus, the more you realize how much God loves you, and He has prepared a home for you in Heaven (John 14:3).

It's also healthier to give up control.
Being the boss can be stressful.
We have enough to worry about
without taking over God's job.

You might be asking what exactly does it mean to surrender. It means you wait on God's timing, and you trust Him to get you through any circumstance.

We tend to be selfish and want our own way. It goes back to that control issue we talked about earlier. When we surrender, our skin crawls because it feels unnatural. And once we make the decision to give it all to God, the devil will use any means to attack, including having family and friends go after you with hurtful words. But if you hold tight, it will get easier.

It's also healthier to give up control. Being the boss can be stressful. We have enough to worry about without taking over God's job. The more you give your Father to handle, the more relaxed you will become.

Funny how we fight giving control to God, yet we allow people and situations to control us all the time.

I know you're shaking your head right now saying "Not me." But it's true.

Don't you recall that time your son got a bad grade on his English paper? You went crazy. And the day your boss didn't give you that raise you deserved. It put you in a bad mood for weeks. How did you behave the last time you were made to wait in a long line at the grocery store or got stuck in a traffic jam? In those instances, you allowed other people and situations to control your emotions.

Embrace God's plan for you. Whatever it is, you will find peace and joy, even in traffic.

Reverend David DePra, writer of "The Good News" blog, describes surrender as this, "I will let God do in me whatever is necessary to get Himself glory, and whatever is necessary to make me into the person He is after."

It's hard for independent women to give up power to another, especially if it's a male figure-head. If you grew up with men in your life who harmed you, it makes it even more difficult. I still find it hard to trust men after being molested by my grandfather. This was a man who should have cared more for me than his own needs but didn't.

When you're hurt that deep, it's hard to trust a patriarchal God.

It took a long time and a lot of Bible reading before I realized God was nothing like my alcoholic father or perverted grandfather. I no longer doubt God's love for me. I finally feel He has my best interests, but the control issues still exist.

God is readily available to take the reins of your life. All you have to do is hand them over to him. Let him control the wild horses.

Don't be afraid of what's in front of you. Just know that when you step out, God will be there to catch you before you sink. Step from the boat and accept all God has to offer.

Are you ready to forget the past and move forward with a deeper relationship with your heavenly Father?

If so, say out loud to God, "I'm all yours, Father."

The reason why many are still troubled,
still seeking, still making little forward progress
is because they haven't yet come
to the end of themselves.
We're still trying to give orders,
and interfering with God's work within us.
—*A.W. Tozer*[liii]

Grab a little God Bling

Though we are incomplete,
God loves us completely.
Though we are imperfect,
He loves us perfectly.
Though we may feel lost
and without compass,
God's love encompasses us completely.
... He loves every one of us,
even those who are flawed, rejected,
awkward, sorrowful, or broken.
—*Dieter F. Uchtdorf,*
Author of
The Remarkable Soul of a Woman[liv]

I never thought I could love anyone as much as my first child. Then my second daughter came along. There's no love deeper than a mother's love. Except maybe a grandmother's. It's amazing how much love we carry in our hearts.

God carries even more.

His love is wonderful, awesome, and unconditional. 1 Corinthians 13:4-6 tells us, "Love is patient, love is kind. It does not envy, it does not boast, it is not proud. It does not dishonor others, it is not self-seeking, it is not easily angered, it keeps no record of wrongs. Love does not delight in evil but rejoices with the truth. It always protects, always trusts, always perseveres."

That is God's love for you. Patient, kind, everlasting.

His love is so vast, it is incomprehensible. He loves us in spite of our selfishness and lack of self-control. He is right there with His love readily available.

God didn't just get stuck with us like birth parents with their children. In Ephesians 1:4, it says "For he chose us in him before the creation of the world to be holy and blameless in his sight." We were each chosen to be one of His daughters. Isn't that awesome? Your Father picked you to be His child.

Not growing up in a loving home, some days it was hard to remember I was loved, much less that God loved me. I'd been a Christian for a while when one day I was driving my forty-minute commute to work and a love song came on the radio. I can't recall which anymore, but that's not important. I just remember thinking how nice it would be to be loved like that.

Then clear as a bell, a voice said, "I love you like that."

I instantly knew it was God. My eyes started tearing up, and a warm feeling swelled in the pit of my stomach. It was the first time in my life I was absolutely sure I was loved. The other commuters probably thought I was nuts doing seventy brushing tears from my eyes. But it was the most glorious sensation I'd ever felt before.

Anytime I start to get down, I think back to that moment of pure joy and love.

God's love.
It's wonderful.
It's awesome.
It's unconditional.

David DePra describes being a child of God as, "A son or daughter of God is one who is walking under the on-going dynamic of Jesus as Lord. They have not only surrendered their life to Christ – their lot in life and all of the details – but they have given THEMSELVES to Jesus as Lord. In short, the Holy Spirit has a growing freedom to do in that person whatever is God's will." As His daughters, in the true sense of the word, we have to give ourselves to Him totally. No longer will we belong to this world. We will now belong to God.

We exist through Him as stated in 1 Corinthians 8:6: "yet for us there is but one God, the Father, from whom all things came and for whom we live; and there is but one Lord, Jesus Christ, through whom all things came and through whom we live." True faith knows that no matter what you're going through, Jesus is right there beside you with His arms wrapped around you. Don't lose sight of Him during hard times, because there is nothing worse than knowing you are alone.

As God's daughter, you'll still have hardships, but you will feel the closeness of your Father from here on in. A sense of peace will come over you every time you think about Him holding your hand.

The more time you spend with Him, the more you'll come to realize His love for you. Unlike some earthly fathers, God will never desert, harm, or neglect. He will always be there to hold you when you need it. Just lift your hand to him. He's right there waiting.

It's time now to enjoy life to the fullest knowing you are the daughter of the greatest King.

We should be astonished
at the goodness of God,
stunned that He should bother
to call us by name,
our mouths wide open at His love,
bewildered that at this very moment
we are standing on holy ground.
—*Brennan Manning,*
Author of The Ragamuffin Gospel:
Good News for the Bedraggled
Beat-Up, and Burnt Out[lvi]

Proof of God's love

God's love for us is never ending. We can't even fathom how much he loves us. The following Psalm gives us constant reminders of God's love.

Psalm 136

Praise the LORD! He is good.
God's love never fails.
Praise the God of all gods.
God's love never fails.
Praise the Lord of lords.
God's love never fails.
Only God works great miracles.[a]
God's love never fails.
With wisdom he made the sky.
God's love never fails.
The Lord stretched the earth
over the ocean.
God's love never fails.
He made the bright lights
in the sky.
God's love never fails.
He lets the sun rule each day.
God's love never fails.
He lets the moon and the stars
rule each night.
God's love never fails.

There are twenty-six verses in Psalm 136, but I only gave you nine. But in each of these, you get nine "God's love never fails." If you read the remainder, you will see that it states twenty-six times that "God's love never fails."

His love is a constant, something we can't get much these days. And His love is not just for anybody, it's for His children. You and me.

Closing Prayer

Father God,

Thank You for loving me so much I can't even fathom. I accept you fully, not just as God and Creator, but as my Father. It is wonderful to know that the God of this world thinks of me often and considers me His child. I pray You continue to help me see Your love in my life daily. Hold on to me, Lord, and get me through the hard times knowing that You are right there beside me. You are an awesome and wonderful God and truly loving Father.
In Jesus' name,
Amen

To Dig Deeper:

A. Here are some questions to help you dig a bit deeper into your relationship with God.

1. Were you ever compared to someone while you were growing up? How did it make you feel? Maybe someone was compared to you. Knowing that comparisons aren't fair, and not realistic, if you could see that person today, what would you say to them?

2. I have a tendency to work out problems before they even occur. I just know that person who I have to deal with is going to give me a hard time, so I play out the scenario in my mind. It, of course, never occurs the way I picture, but that hasn't stopped me from doing it. The funny part is, it's never as bad as I think it's going to be. How do you deal with upcoming issues? Have you ever been in a situation you thought was going to be worse than it actually was? Why do you think we try to work things out before the event instead of just giving it up to Jesus in the first place?

3. I moved from Idaho to Florida when I was about twenty-years-old. The only person I knew was the friend I came with. While I was running away, because I found myself pregnant and unmarried, something inside said it was the right step. What has been the biggest leap of faith you've ever taken? Are you glad you did? Why or why not?

4. Growing up, my mom forced me to take my little sister with me when I played with my friends. Needless to say, I didn't enjoy it much. Were you ever forced to spend time with someone you didn't want do? Or were you the tag-along? How did it feel? How is it knowing God wants to spend time with you?

5. Write a list of five of your best attributes. Now ask a friend to tell you what they think are five of the best things about you. Are the lists the same? Why do you think that is?

6. We read, in part, Bible verse Psalm 136 at the end of the chapter. Read the Psalm in its entirety. How do you feel knowing God's love will never fail or disappear?

B. Read the following Bible verses. How do they touch you?

1. Galatians 6:4-5: "Each one should test their own actions. Then they can take pride in themselves alone, without comparing themselves to someone else, for each one should carry their own load."
   a. Have you ever had to take on someone else's load, maybe at work, or as a child for another sibling? How did it make you feel at the time? How do you feel about it now?

   b. I picture when I get to Heaven they'll be a waiting room where one of God's angels will go over my "goods" and "bads." Maybe they'll be kept in a two-drawer filing cabinet in the corner of the room. I have a feeling the "bad" drawer will hold a lot more than the other. What one thing have you done that you would like to see disappear from your "bad" filing drawer in Heaven? What will be the one thing you're proudest of in your "good" drawer?

2. Psalm 27:1-3: "The Lord is my light and my salvation—whom shall I fear? The Lord is the stronghold of my life—of whom shall I be afraid? When the wicked advance against me to devour me, it is my enemies and my foes who will stumble and fall. Though an army besiege me, my heart will not fear; though war break out against me, even then I will be confident."

a.It's easy for us as humans to fear things, sometimes irrationally. I have acrophobia – the extreme fear of heights. Some people have Hylophobia – the fear of trees. What is the one thing you fear most? Why do you think we fear things to the point of being irrational about them?

b. Have you ever been in a situation where you feared you would be harmed? How did you deal with that situation?

3. Psalm 145:17-18: "The Lord is righteous in all his ways and faithful in all he does. The Lord is near to all who call on him, to all who call on him in truth."

a. God is faithful. He does what He says He's going to do. Humans have an issue with keeping their word. When was the last time you made a promise you didn't keep? Was there a good excuse or did you just changed your mind? If you could go back, would you now keep that promise?

b. It's easy in this day and age to contact people by text, instant message, or phone call. A dear friend of mine lost track of her son for years. He was an alcoholic and became homeless. Thankfully, he's okay today, but I can't imagine not knowing where one of my children was for that length of time. When was the last time you were desperate to speak to someone you couldn't reach? How did you react? How does it feel to know that God is right there with you at all times?

4. Galations 2:21: "I have been crucified with Christ and I no longer live, but Christ lives in me. The life I now live in the body, I live by faith in the Son of God, who loved me and gave himself for me. I do not set aside the grace of God, for if righteousness could be gained through the law, Christ died for nothing!"

a. This verse talks about Christ living in us. When was the last time you purposely showed Jesus to another either through your actions or your words?

b. Jesus died a very painful death for our sins, not His. Other than a child or close relative, is there anyone you'd be willing to die for in such a painful way?

5. Isaiah 64:8 tells us, "Yet you, LORD, are our Father. We are the clay, you are the potter; we are all the work of your hand."

a. We are never completed, always working toward perfection. God formed us in our mother's womb (Jeremiah 1:15), and He continues to work with us our entire life. Do you ever get tired of not being "finished" yet?

b. Picture God at a potter's wheel forming you with his hands. Write down all the images that come to your mind.

CHAPTER FIVE
Accepting His Love

Come to me,
all of you who are tired
from carrying heavy loads,
and I will give you rest.
—*Matthew 11:28*

———————

Now that we've been through the issues caused to a daughter by an emotionally and/or physically absent father, let's go into how God is the best replacement. As we've gone along, we've found ways to work around some of these abandonment issues, but now is the time to see why you should choose God. And why calling Him father will draw you into a deeper relationship.

I should warn you that once you start your journey bad things will occur. The car will break down, friends will pick fights, family members will leave. It's all Satan's doing. He'll do anything to force a wedge between you and God.

However, perseverance in God's word can help you through.

There will be high times when you feel God's presence near you, and other times you might think He's walked away. You will have valleys – a loss of a loved one, losing a job, losing a home. Then there are the ruts that occur in your everyday life. An argument between you and your child, your boss' bad mood, and the steaks burning on the grill.

If you keep a close walk with Jesus, you can get through all these things with a modicum of self-control. All because you have a loving, godly father to hold onto.

Too often we allow control or vulnerability to keep us from accepting God fully, but the more you come to know Him, the more you'll understand His plans for you, and even why you might have had your father-daughter issues. The more you count on God, the stronger you will become in your faith. No matter what you've gone through, in the end, God has your best interests in mind.

He wants his daughters to feel loved, no matter the circumstances we might face. Our Father wants to heal our hurt and give us support during our trials. Anytime we need Him, He is there, with his hands outstretched. All we have to do is come to Him.

Once you realize He has been there for you since before you were born that love you desire will come rushing in. But make sure you have tissues near when you get the realization. Trust me, you'll need them to wipe the tears of joy from your face.

———

To be comforted by God
is a promise that few of us ever receive,
because we are consumed
with controlling our situations
to avoid being vulnerable.
—E'yen A. Gardner
Author of
Humbly Submitting to Chang
– The Wilderness Experience[lvii]

———

Through His Eyes

The best way to get rid
of the negative thoughts
is to crowd them out
with something else bigger
and more beautiful
worship of the One who holds everything
in His powerful and capable hands.
—Jocelyn Green, author of
Faith Deployed...Again:
More Daily Encouragement
for Military Wives[lviii]

How many of you have preteen or teenage daughters? Have you ever heard one say hateful things about themselves? Girls are especially notorious for this more so than boys. They say things like "I'm so fat," or "I'm ugly." We scoff at the notion. It's like they're seeing someone different in the mirror than you are.

How many times have you ever said those same words or similar hateful things about yourself? Do you think God perceives you the same way you do yourself? No more than you do your own child. When we say something hateful about ourselves, He's taken aback because He doesn't see what we see.

That's because we view ourselves through the eyes of our own experience. If we're prone to acne or pimples, we're more likely to focus on looks whereas someone who has trouble keeping weight off will focus on their body issues.

No matter how much weight I've lost over the years (actually down to the 120's at one time), I still see myself as fat. That's why diseases like anorexia nervosa are so prevalent in this country. These women don't observe skin and bones, they only notice the one ounce of fat on their bodies. A dangerous disease perpetrated by the hate we feel inside.

For daughters who grew up without a good father figure, all they see is someone in the mirror not worthy of love. She can't be special if Dad never thought she was.

It's hard when you've lived feeling unloved to believe you can be considered God's daughter and that you are worthy of His love. We tend to find it hard to not trust in verses like John 1:12-13 which tell us, "Yet to all who did receive him, to those who believed in his name, he gave the right to become children of God—children born not of natural descent, nor of human decision or a husband's will, but born of God."

We ignore verses that tell of our inheritance by being adopted by God like Ephesians 1:13-14 which says, "And you also were included in Christ when you heard the message of truth, the gospel of your salvation. When you believed, you were marked in him with a seal, the promised Holy Spirit, who is a deposit guaranteeing our inheritance until the redemption of those who are God's possession—to the praise of his glory."

Like a loving father, God doesn't want to lose any of us to drugs or despair. Jesus explains that He was sent to save us in John 6:39-40, "'And this is the will of him who sent me, that I shall lose none of all those he has given me, but raise them up at the last day. For my Father's will is that everyone who looks to the Son and believes in him shall have eternal life, and I will raise them up at the last day.'"

You can never run far enough to not find God there beside you. Nothing can take you away from Him.

And, in order to be His fully, we need to be born again. We need to change our actions and thoughts, including how we view ourselves. We are no longer some fat little kid dad wanted nothing to do with. We are now daughters of a wonderful and loving King.

> When those old feelings of rejection come in,
> we feel stressed, unblessed, and depressed.

But, how can you trust fully in someone you aren't sure is trustworthy?

The quick answer is by reading Bible verses like those above and having faith that what you read is true. The more we read them, the more we'll believe them.

The following are more verses that show how God loves His children.

1. God thinks about you. In Jeremiah 29:11 He tells us, "'For I know the plans I have for you,' declares the LORD, 'plans to prosper you and not to harm you, plans to give you hope and a future.'"

2. God will bless you. Proverbs 8:21, "bestowing a rich inheritance on those who love me and making their treasuries full."

3. He never changes according to Hebrews 13:8, which says, "Jesus Christ is the same yesterday and today and forever."

4. You will never comprehend how great He loves you. Ephesians 3:19, "and to know this love that surpasses knowledge—that you may be filled to the measure of all the fullness of God."

No amount of "I love yous" from others can fix the pain of the past. That healing can only come from God.

Even if the memory of your father's abandonment fades, the rejection doesn't. In fact, it grows with each new rejection. Each time someone says something that makes you feel unloved or not good enough, those old issues come bounding back to the forefront of our minds.

Sometimes it's not really even rejection, but our perception of the situation.

For instance, when my oldest used to take our granddaughter to visit my ex-husband, some of those self-hateful words slipped through. Words like "She loves him more." I should be happy they have a good relationship, but a voice inside would tell me she was choosing him over me. It's not true, but some days the devil gets to me as well. He hits in the heart where he knows it will hurt the most.

When those old feelings of rejection come in, we feel stressed, unblessed, and depressed. The only thing we want to do is crawl back under the covers.

You want to follow Jesus by doing onto others as you would have them do to you. Then the boss comes in and blames you for something another co-worker did. He doesn't care to listen to explanations. You want to be a good Christian woman, always smiling, but instead a few choice words come to mind. Not Godly ones either. The "do unto others" mantra ends right there.

Then we hate ourselves for feeling these emotions. The insecurities flood in. No amount of arguing can convince us we're God's daughter. We see ourselves as failures, as unable to be loved because we are imperfect.

We're told God loves us, and He sees us different from the way we see ourselves, however we allow our emotions to speak over what the Bible tells us, what others say, and what Jesus' experienced on the cross that proved God's love is true.

Not only did God love you enough to come to earth in the form of a human and die for you, but He wants a personal relationship with you. We have to take a step forward and show Him we want the same. The love you feel when you give yourself totally to God the Father will release those inner demons of your past. It's time to take His hand in yours and start your walk toward freedom from the self-hate you keep inside.

Our greatest glory is not in never falling
but in rising every time we fall.
—*Confucius*
Chinese Philosopher[lix]

How Low Can I Go?

God's word promises us
that we will survive the valleys
because Jesus is with us.
And, if we stay close to him,
we will produce much fruit –
the kind that will last.
—Henriet Schapelhouman[lx]

Have you ever got out of bed, feeling good only to have something occur that destroyed your good mood? Maybe the kids started arguing or one got ill?

Life comes with ups and downs. Some parts lower than others. Most Christians refer to them as valleys.

We often think of valleys as being a time of illness, death, or divorce. However, we probably go through a rough patch every single day. We just don't realize they are valleys because these problems don't last for extended periods of time. Valleys are not necessarily long, drawn out torture. They can be something as simple as someone cursing you out on the telephone at work. It is anything that can take away your joy. Some are deep holes, some are canyons, but most are just ruts along the road.

It's these ruts that tear at your joy each day.

When we're sitting on top of the mountain, we believe nothing bad can ever happen. We focus on the good, at times giving ourselves credit for getting there, instead of God. Yet, all it takes is one small rumble to toss us from that great view.

Imagine what would happen if you went to work only to find the company has closed. It's happened. People find themselves not just out of a job, but with no final paycheck either.

Where is this loving father everyone's been talking about at these times? The Bible says God doesn't want us to suffer, yet here we are, afraid of what's coming next. Most of the time, our suffering is not God's doing. The devil is the cause of a lot of our pain. And pain also comes when we sin.

When something bad occurs, we need to try to find the good. For instance, let's say it's . . .

The loss of a job: Time to find one you'll enjoy, spend more time with your family, or go back to school so you can get a better paying job.

Major surgery: A harsh reminder to exercise more, and your recuperation period allows more time to spend with God.

The death of a child: A child's death is perhaps one of the hardest realities of life, but try to look on your child as a gift that you had for a short period of time. Then once their visit here on Earth has ended, they headed back to God. In time, you will be with them again.

Now don't get me wrong, I'm no Pollyanna. Most of the time, I see the glass as half-empty and there's lipstick on the rim of the glass. Not my shade either. But in tragedies like these, in order to work through the pain and fear, we have to reach for God's light or depression can settle in. It's like you've fallen into a large canyon, and you can't crawl out. Remember at those times, God is at the top holding a rope. You just need to grab on.

It's normal to believe at times of tragedies that God has left you. We have a tendency to allow our circumstances and emotions to take control during a tragic event. Toss in a past of paternal rejection and/ or abandonment and look out.

By staying focused on God, we can learn to tell whether these emotions are deceiving us by making things appear worse than they truly are. Maybe it's not really that major of a situation, but we're allowing fear to take over.

When things get real bad, we might shut down our feelings to try to ease some of our pain. The trauma of losing someone you love, especially if it was a father at an early age, can shape how you see relationships forever. You might have shut yourself down in order to not feel the pain from the loss whether it was because he died at an early age or abandoned you.

This valley can be so deep it keeps you closed up from allowing other emotions to enter.

Then there's the other end of the spectrum where you feel too much. Even minor setbacks send you into a blubbering mess. The drama queen comes out, and no one has ever had it any worse.

No matter how bad things might get, we need to keep telling ourselves this valley is only temporary. In the end, we'll find ourselves pain-free in God's arms, sitting at the table with Jesus. Deuteronomy 31:8 reminds us that "The Lord himself goes before you and will be with you; he will never leave you nor forsake you. Do not be afraid; do not be discouraged."

It's natural to want all the highs without the lows, but no one is exempt from trials. Not even the best Christian. Without ordeals, how will we know it's really God you're relying on and not ourselves or our circumstances? How will we grow in our faith?

Think about a loving father. If he were to give his child everything they desired, including keeping them from heartbreak, how would their world be? In fact, some kids these days live in this realm. They feel entitled, they get a trophy just for participating, and as they become adults, they don't adjust well. If they lose a promotion or even if their candidate loses an election, they have a tendency to withdraw and have a hard time coping. Our society has almost done away with the two most important things to hang onto during tragedies – good men/fathers and God.

Our pain is where we can meet
and connect deeper with God.

How many times has a natural disaster struck and some non-believer said, "So, where was your God?" He's right beside you and everyone else, holding on to us. He warned there would be highs and lows. James 1:12 reads, "Blessed is the one who perseveres under trial because, having stood the test, that person will receive the crown of life that the Lord has promised to those who love him."

When we hit hard times, we either turn more to God or away from Him. At times of tragedies, God is the only way out. I can't help but feel bad for people who turn to Christ expecting their lives to be spectacular. At the first bump in the road, these fair-weather Christians leave and blast God for all their problems. However, hardships are an essential part of growth. We don't always grow during good times. It's during these hard times that we show our true faith and courage. Most of us wouldn't grow in Jesus if we only lived on the mountain peak.

Pain is where we connect deeper with God. During something bad, we need someone to hold onto. As a child it's usually a parent we trust. If you never had that father-figure, you can feel truly alone and not know how to handle the situation. That's when God is most important. He's there to give you that much needed support we don't find elsewhere.

Nothing in the Bible can prepare you for a complete commitment to Jesus Christ. It takes suffering to realize you are totally relying on your Savior and to realize that His promise to never leave is true. These dark times can be unpredictable. We don't know how long they will last or the outcome. Our Heavenly Father is our lifeline in times of need.

We have to be willing to live without a net. The more we depend on God during our dark times, the deeper our foundation of faith will become so we won't roll from that mountain during the next tragedy.

If you take your eyes off Him, you could end up like Peter when he stepped out of the boat in Matthew 14:29-30. "And He said, 'Come!' And Peter got out of the boat, and walked on the water and came toward Jesus. But seeing the wind, he became frightened and beginning to sink…" He was able to walk on the water until He took his eyes off Jesus. You can be a Peter and walk on water as long as you keep focused on Jesus so you don't drown in a mire of anger and despair. No matter how dark the situation is you're going through, eventually you will see the light, because valleys are only temporary. If you allow your pain to take over your life, you can get into all types of emotional messes like bitterness and self-pity.

These tests make us realize how much we desire a savior. Something to hold on to that is far greater than we are. During these valleys, read positive scripture to keep focused on God's love and the fact that you are not alone. Trust such verses as Joshua 1:9 which reads, "Have I not commanded you? Be strong and courageous. Do not be frightened, and do not be dismayed, for the Lord your God is with you wherever you go."

Satan will use your feelings of abandonment to make you think God has left the way your father did. But God has always been a constant in your life, and His promises are true. Just hold tight to His hand and feel His loving arms wrap around you in time of need. You'll eventually be able to climb back up the side of that mountain, no matter how slippery the slope.

———

My philosophy is:
Life is hard, but God is good.
Try not to confuse the two.
—*Anne F. Beiler,*
founder of Auntie Anne's Pretzels[lxi]

———

Big Girls Don't Cry

Let your tears come.
Let them water your soul.
—*Eileen Mayhew, Writer*[lxii]

———

Have you ever felt so alone in your pain you don't believe anyone understood what you were going through? That's despair. It can be one of the loneliest places to live.

The city of Despair is an isolated location where no one understands another's pain, and no one seems to care what the other is going through.

Growing up in an unloving situation can make it hard to realize you're not alone.

To this day, I still have issues with asking for help from others. I'm so used to dealing with things on my own, I find it hard to share with others if something goes wrong. I can ask for prayer for my children and friends, but hardly do so for myself, no matter the circumstances.

Women are used to being the fixers. We are the moms who make the kids feel better when they're sick. We keep the house in order, however some things we can't repair. Certain circumstances make us want to stop, curl back under the covers and forget life. Unfortunately, a lot of women turn to drugs, alcohol, even suicide when despair hits.

We have a tendency to forget God is the gentle voice that whispers "Just one more step. Tomorrow will be better."

Most of us turn to our friends, even social media all the while crying about our loss instead of God. But He wants you to turn to Him first. And He doesn't mind the crying. In fact God wants you to come when you're at your most vulnerable.

A lot of people hate to admit they come to the breaking point where they cry, but it's okay. Let it out. I don't mean a few sobs, I mean let the tears fall. A good cry can release a lot of stress and tension. When it's over, you feel cleansed. You might even find the circumstances not as bad as you thought.

When you've got the blues, the more you cry, the better you feel. Keeping everything bottled up can cause anxiety, nervousness, and stress. Tension fills our bodies when we're sad. Crying releases all that pressure.

Crying is like "emotional perspiration," a phrase coined by New York Times reporter Benedict Carey. When you cry out to God, you allow healing waters to wash over you. When you're hurting, and you don't know what to say, you only need to say one word to be heard – Jesus.

When you come to the realization that your relationship with your father will never be repaired, it can hurt. Don't hold it in. Allow the tears to wash you clean. Let God know your pain and sadness in not having a good relationship with your Earthly father. Then once the tears have dried up, thank God for being the father you never had, because He has always been with you.

Nothing is better than when we fall on our faces, open our hearts, and pour out all our emotions to our loving Father. At that point, we're giving up any pretense of being in charge. We are allowing ourselves a wave of sadness followed by relief in knowing God will take care of us.

In the Bible, the Israelites were constantly crying out to God. Every time they found themselves captured, they cried out. Jesus also cried out to God. Hebrews 5:7 states, "During the days of Jesus' life on earth, he offered up prayers and petitions with fervent cries and tears to the one who could save him from death, and he was heard because of his reverent submission." If Jesus, the only perfect being to exist on this earth cried for relief, who are we to not do the same?

We have a tendency to forget
God is the gentle voice that whispers
"Just one more step. Tomorrow will be better."

There is no shame in asking for help. A true father is to listen no matter how long you cry, plead, or beg. This is another way God proves His love. Whatever pain you're going through, picture His gentle hand on your back or your head against his chest. That image alone should give you comfort.

We've all had bad days. Things that send us to the edge. Whether it be illness, money issues, death of a loved one, or a marriage falling apart. Life can be a pressure cooker about to explode. It takes all our power just to get out of bed in the morning. This is the time you MUST lean on God the most. The Lord can repair, mend, or change how you face circumstances. Pray for Him to get you through. Pray for His grace and mercy. And don't be afraid to cry.

Like a loving father, God doesn't like to see His children suffer. Our Father never gives us more than we can handle. Galatians 6:9 reminds us to "not grow weary of doing good, for in due season we will reap, if we do not give up."

Some days I wonder if God thinks I'm Superwoman with all He gives me to deal with. I'm sure you feel the same. But I know He's right there beside me, holding my hand along the way. And He's there with you too. No matter what, He'll get you through to the other side.

So don't be afraid to cry out to Him. He will hold you and comfort you. Who knows, He might even bring the tissues to dry your eyes.

The soul would have no rainbow
had the eyes no tears.
—*John Vance Cheney, Poet*[lxiv]

Stop the Hate

Thou canst not think worse of me
than I do of myself.
—*Robert Burton*[lxv]

It's a proven fact that what you say about yourself, you come to believe. Say you're stupid, you'll start to fail in school. Say you're a loser, and you'll never win at any game. A lot of our self-hate comes from our childhood. We drag our baggage from our past into our adulthood.

Daughters without a good father relationship believe they are unlovable because their dad didn't know how to show love. And these women end up berating themselves for what is lacking in their lives.

The best way to move away from your past is to allow God to move in your life. That means spending time with Him. We only get good at something when we practice. The more time we spend with God, the more we'll call on Him in time of strife, and the more we'll realize His word is truer than the voices in our head.

Some of us not only have trouble allowing God all the way in, but with implementing any plan to draw closer to Him.

If you are having a hard time finding ways to get into that father/daughter relationship with God, see if the following doesn't help:

1. Write a prayer or letter to God. Tell Him your doubts, fears, but also remember to thank Him for all He's done for you. Include any expectations you have of this new relationship with God the Father.

2. Another way to draw closer to God is by reading your Bible daily. There are several websites that tell you how to read the Bible in one year like www.Biblestudytools.com and www.christianity.com. Or you can chose to study the New Testament or certain chapters like Psalms and/or Proverbs.

The best way to block self-condemnation
is to repeat the truth over and over.
You are loved. You are worth love.

---

3. Another way is with journaling. Some people find it helpful to put their blessings and hardships down on paper. If this works for you, do so.

4. Pray. Find a peaceful place and talk with God. Allow Him to sooth your mind.

5. Everybody is different. Some people need to see the Word in order to absorb it, others do better by hearing it. People who need to hear in order to "get" it might do better listening to sermons on YouTube or purchasing audio Bibles or Bible studies.

The point is to find what works for you.
The more you read about God's love, the deeper you will experience it. Also, practice telling yourself daily that you are loved. Practice looking in the mirror and saying "I am loved" several times. You might feel unease at first, but eventually it will become natural.

And the more you say it, the more it becomes real.

The best way to block self-condemnation is to repeat the truth over and over. You are loved. You are worth love.

The more your grow in your faith, the easier it'll be to listen to the whispers of God and have the peace as stated in Romans 5:1: "Therefore, since we have been justified through faith, we have peace with God through our Lord Jesus Christ." And isn't peace a lot more pleasant than distress?

Practice is the hardest part of learning,
and training is the essence of transformation.
—Ann Voskamp,
Christian author[lxvi]

Let Your Faith Echo

Every mountain top is within reach
if you just keep climbing.
—Barry Finlay
Author of Kilimanjaro
and Beyond[lxvii]

Some days I'll be going along fine, then something will occur to bring me down. My sister will call regarding the bad day she's having, and I'm not very patient about it. Calling when I'm busy to discuss a problem with her latest boyfriend drives me crazy. We don't live near each other so I've never met these guys, and quite frankly, to me, they're always the same issues. Just writing about it I could feel my mood change, and I don't know why.

Do you have something in your life that does the same thing to you?

I seem to have more patience with my friends over the same issues than her. It probably has a lot to do with my childhood. I can't help but wonder if she feels the same way about me.

Whenever I have to deal with such issues, I sense I've lost my walk and wonder why God continually puts up with me.

It's because He loves me. And He loves you too. We've seen proof in the Bible.

Unlike me, He'll never be too busy with another member of His family, and He'll never treat you like you're unworthy of His time.

If we could only take all our emotions and turn them into love for the Father, our lives would be one of peace.

However, having grown up unable to trust the one man in your life you should have been able to, it can be hard to fully trust God. He understands that. And He wants you to tell Him you're having these difficulties.

You might even question how a loving father can allow His children to suffer with tragedies. Realize some things that take place are not God's will. Remember the Lord's prayer we prayed in the first chapter? It states emphatically that God wants His will to be done on earth as it is in Heaven. There is no pain in Heaven, so it only makes sense that He would like there to be no pain here on Earth as well.

Still, God wants to hear your doubts in Him. How can He fix what's wrong if you don't tell Him?

Some problems are way beyond our capacity to deal with. Illness, the death of someone we love, losing our home. That's why prayer is so important. There's nothing like seeing a woman go through chemotherapy with a smile on her face to know she's truly relying on God. And isn't it better for a wife to fall down on her knees praying because of a cheating husband instead of trashing him on social media?

God is like that protective liquid,
trying to help us
through the irritants in our lives.

Dealing with pitfalls in life isn't always easy, but God is there with arms wide open anytime we need Him. And He loves nothing more than for his daughters to turn to Him for help. Isn't that why we want so desperately to have that father-daughter relationship? So we have someone other than ourselves to depend on?

We find it easy to shout God's praises when we're on the mountain top, but God wants to hear those praises when we're in the valley as well. That's where it echoes the loudest.

Remember the story of Job? He lost everything, but no matter how bad things got for him, he never cursed God. In Job 2:9, "his wife even suggested he curse God and drop dead." Job's response in 2:10 was, 'You are talking like a foolish woman. Shall we accept good from God, and not trouble?' In all this, Job did not sin in what he said." Too many times, we get mad at God for the bad, forgetting the good He's provided.

There will always be trials and testing in our lives. Some large, like breast cancer, some small like spaghetti sauce on your blouse during an important business dinner. At the time it may seem humongous, but in the scheme of things it's not. However, if too many of these small disasters occur at one time, we feel as if our world is out of control. Just remember, during hard times we can either grow or wither. Holding onto God will help us grow.

Our true heart becomes evident when times are difficult. Will we trust God or run from Him? The choice to stay or go is ours.

If you're going through a trying time right now, think of yourself as an oyster with a pearl. The pearl begins as some sort of irritant to the oyster. He secretes a liquid over and over to sooth the ache the irritant has caused. In time, these layers become the pearl. God is like that protective liquid, trying to help us through the irritants in our lives. Layer by layer, he builds our character so we are no longer the lost lamb we were when we first came to Him. The more we allow God to seals his protection over us, the more we become a treasure.

And please don't be afraid to share any of your problems with your Christian sisters. That's what they're there for, to hold you up when you're falling down.

By showing others how we rely on God the Father, we announce that we are not alone. That strength others see in us is encouraging. It makes them want to know our God. It's not easy to come through a crisis without faith. I imagine nonbelievers feel very alone at times when things are the hardest.

Relying on God gets us through even the scariest times in our lives. As we learn to lean on Him when things are running smoothly, we will automatically reach for Him when times get hard. With God, the depth of the valley might not be as deep as it seems. And His love will keep you from feeling truly alone during difficult times.

The next time you find yourself going through a tragedy or just a rut in the road, reach your hand up. Experience the warmth of His fingers as they cover yours until you're pulled back up to an even plateau.

It is only in sorrow bad weather masters us;
in joy we face the storm and defy it.
—*Amelia Barr, Writer*[lxviii]

More Proof of God's Love

Do you remember the song Jesus Loves Me (This I Know)? The next words are "for the Bible tells me so." The Bible is full of passages where God shows proof of His love for us. Psalm 103:7-12 gives us some insight into this deep love.

Psalm 103:7-12

He made known his ways to Moses,
his deeds to the people of Israel:
The LORD is compassionate and gracious,
slow to anger, abounding in love.
He will not always accuse,
nor will he harbor his anger forever;
he does not treat us as our sins deserve
or repay us according to our iniquities.
For as high as the heavens are above the earth,
so great is his love for those who fear him;
as far as the east is from the west,
so far has he removed our transgressions from us

There are so many lines that show God's love for us in this section. "He is compassionate and gracious," and "He does not treat us as our sins deserve" are just two such verses. A cruel God would offer no forgiveness or compassion for His people. But we worship a loving God, a loving Father.

It is sometimes hard for us to wrap our minds around the fact that God loves us so much He wants to have a close relationship, but He does. We just have to be willing to accept it.

Closing Prayer

Dear Father,

I trust You, Lord. I trust You to get me through my pain. Please take hold of me when I feel there is no moving forward because I hurt so much. Whisper to me that You are there and always have been. Remind me I have never been alone. Thank You for holding on to me during my trying times. I will always keep You near as You have kept me near to You.
In Jesus name,
Amen

To **Dig Deeper:**

A. Here are some questions to help you dig a bit deeper into your relationship with God.

1. We have all had times where we've had a bad day and then something funny occurs to make us laugh. Maybe our child says something so unbelievably funny that we can't help but smile. I believe that's God trying to ease our tension. What was one of the funniest times you can recall that gave you that much needed break in tension?

2. Years ago, my youngest daughter and I were in a car accident. I was at a stop light and a man slammed into us from behind. He hit us once, bounced off, and hit us again. In front of me was a young man on a motorcycle, and in front of him was another car. I'd been trying to get home that night, but obstacles kept me from being able to leave on time. If I hadn't been at that light, there's a chance the motorcyclist might have died. I also believe the people who weren't able to get tickets on the Titanic weren't so disappointed a couple days later. Have you ever had a situation where God put obstacles in your way to keep you from doing something you wanted and it turned out to be a blessing? Did you remember to thank God for delaying your trip?

3. We all have low points in lives where misery takes over. Think about the lowest point in your past. Now that you look back, can you see any blessings that came from it? Do you see the situation in the same light?

4. I'm one of those who refuses to cry in public. I'll try anything. Yet, I find I start to tear up more easily now that I have God in my life - mostly joyful tears. How easy is it for you to cry in front of others? When was the last time you had a full blown sob fest?

5. We started off this chapter talking about hateful things we say about ourselves. It's always easier to come up with the bad over good. But I want you to take a moment, and write down five of the attributes God might see in you. How did it make you feel to focus on the good instead of the bad?

B. Read the following Bible verses. Reflect on them. How does each show God's love for you?

1. Matthew 11:28-30: "'Come to me, all you who are weary and burdened, and I will give you rest. Take my yoke upon you and learn from me, for I am gentle and humble in heart, and you will find rest for your souls. For my yoke is easy and my burden is light.'"

a. As stated in this passage, God's burden upon us is light. We sometimes put too much pressure on ourselves and that's what weighs us down, but God never gives us more than we can handle. What burden do you need to rid yourself of today? Give it to Jesus and free yourself.

b. This verse shows us how deeply God wants us to rely on Him. Which part of this passage do you find most calming?

2. Romans 8:38-39: "For I am convinced that neither death nor life, neither angels nor demons, neither the present nor the future, nor any powers, neither height nor depth, nor anything else in all creation, will be able to separate us from the love of God that is in Christ Jesus our Lord."

a. It's great knowing God will never stop loving us, no matter what. Has there ever been a time in your life when you thought you loved someone but an event destroyed that love? How did you deal with it at that time? Remembering back, is there sadness, relief, or both that the relationship ended?

b. I'm sure you've watched television shows about people who explore the ocean. Remember Jacque Cousteau? No matter how far he went, Cousteau never reached the bottom. God's love is deeper than any ocean. What's the deepest hole or furthest place (cave, abandoned building) you've entered into? How did it feel with each step you took? Were you scared, excited, a little of both?

3. Psalm 18:6: "In my distress I called to the Lord; I cried to my God for help. From his temple he heard my voice; my cry came before him, into his ears."

a. God hears us when we call out to Him. Has there been a time when you've needed someone and were unable to reach them at the time? How did that make you feel? How does it feel knowing God is there with you always?

b. Imagine the temple where God resides. Describe how you picture it in your mind. What colors are the brightest? What does the throne He sits in look like?

4. Psalm 66:17-20: "I cried out to him with my mouth; his praise was on my tongue. If I had cherished sin in my heart, the Lord would not have listened; but God has surely listened and has heard my prayer. Praise be to God, who has not rejected my prayer or withheld his love from me!"

a. God hears our prayers, but there is a caveat. As stated in the verse above, we must not cherish sin in our hearts. Is there a sin you're hiding deep inside? If so, ask God to forgive you right now so you will be free from it.

b. We often forget to praise God during a rough time because we are so focused on our pain. How often have you cried out to God for help? Did you praise Him in the middle of your turmoil? Why do you think we forget He is there with us during our rough times?

5. Philippians 4:10-13: "I rejoiced greatly in the Lord that at last you renewed your concern for me. Indeed, you were concerned, but you had no opportunity to show it. I am not saying this because I am in need, for I have learned to be content whatever the circumstances. I know what it is to be in need, and I know what it is to have plenty. I have learned the secret of being content in any and every situation, whether well fed or hungry, whether living in plenty or in want. I can do all this through him who gives me strength."

a. In this passage, there is contentment "whatever the circumstance." Often we are not content even when things are going well in our lives. When was the last time you saw something you wanted, but couldn't afford it or were restricted from getting it? How did it feel to know you could not have it? As you've grown older, do you find yourself more content with what you have than when you were younger? Why do you think that is?

b. Is there something in your life that needs to be changed in order for you to feel content? Maybe you're miserable at your job or you're having relationship issues. If so, ask God to help you through. Did you feel more at peace after your prayer? Why do you think that is?

CHAPTER SIX
Allow Your Ponytail
to Swing in the Wind

Snuggle in God's arms.
When you are hurting,
when you feel lonely, left out.
Let Him cradle you, comfort you,
reassure you of
His all-sufficient power and love.
—*Kay Arthur*
Author and co-CEO of
Precept Ministries International[lxix]

Have you ever sat around and watched a group of children play? They don't care about rules or winning. It's about having fun. There's always one girl with long hair put up in a ponytail. When she walks, it swings back and forth on the back of her head. This girl knows what true freedom really means. This is a child who understands that by relying on others (her parents), she has no concerns so she can play without worry. She allows her ponytail to swing in the wind.

Unfortunately, this girl eventually grows up to face the realities of the world. Concerns over finances, family, and her career take over.

And the ponytail ceases to sway. She gave in to worry and anxiety.

All worry does is give you ulcers and make you eat too much chocolate. (Is there such a thing?) That's why giving into God is so important. He can free you from worry and concerns of this world.

Not that every aspect of your life will be worry free. After all, kids get ill, parents grow old, and friends discover lumps. But in the long run, you will lead a more peaceful existence if you just give everything up to God. Knowing He can be totally trusted to help you through, and to never leave you, will give you a peace you've never had before.

Like most fathers, God wants to help. He wants to take away our burdens. We just have to let go.

Picture yourself holding a helium-filled balloon stuffed full of the things that stress you most. The mortgage payment, the boss who is constantly on your back, the SAT your daughter has to take, or squirrels in your attic. Yes, me again.

Hold the string to your balloon between two fingers. Now, open your fingers. Watch your worries float away.

If only it could be so easy to relax and let God take over.

When someone mentions peace and relaxation, what do you picture? Maybe a beautiful sunny day. Or a trip to an island in the Caribbean where you don't work. There might be a hammock swaying between two trees and a drink with an umbrella. A waiter with a nice chiseled chest caters to your every whim. No worries. No stress.

A wonderful dream. Too bad you have to open your eyes and face civilization again.

Unless we earn a billion dollars and retire at an early age very few of us achieve this type of lifestyle.

The best way to have time for Jesus
is to make it.

I thought that would happen when my first fiction book was

released. Boy, was I surprised Breathless didn't hit the New York Times Bestseller's list.

The daily grind of this world tries to keep us focused away from Jesus, but we must persevere. Stay steadfast about making your day around Him, not Him around your day. If there's no time to read the Bible, rearrange your schedule. Instead of eating lunch out with co-workers, spend the time eating and reading. While waiting in the line of cars to get the kids, pull open your Bible. Imagine how much better your mood will be when the children clamor inside the vehicle.

I roll my eyes every time I hear a writer say they don't have time to write, yet they can tell me what happened on that talent show the night before. It's the same with Christians.

Did you watch who won the dance contest last week? Or what the best television show is on TV? If you are more in touch with the popular television shows than you are with Jesus, you need to rearrange a few things in your life.

Okay. I know you need time to unwind. But wouldn't it be better to unwind with God than with some size zero woman walking around on television or some guy who is so chiseled, it's impossible to believe he's real. (In most cases actors aren't any more real than the actresses these days.)

The best way to have time for Jesus is to make it. Set a certain amount of time aside each day to pray and read. Giving God your time shows your love for Him. Isn't that the least we can do after all He's done for us?

No matter how great things seem to be at the moment, there will eventually be challenges to face. The sooner you get started taking time with Jesus, the easier these situations will be. If you allow God to lead, there will be less stress.

Accept your Father's arms for assurance and safety during the storms of life. When tragedy strikes and life seems the hardest, that is when you need to hold on the tightest. Like a child gripping her father's hand at the scary part of a movie, you must grasp God's hand when you are at your lowest point.

There is nothing God can't do, so allow Him to show you how He can make things better. No large screen television, luxury yacht, or vacation with an endless supply of rum will ever make you truly happy. The Lord is the only solution with a lifetime guarantee.

―――――

…WHEN WE acknowledge
God's supreme role in our life
and set our mind on Him,
He enables us to be women of hope.
—*Elizabeth George,*
Bestselling Christian Author[lxx]

―――――

Time to Get Consumed

Come to the edge.
We can't. We're afraid.
Come to the edge.
We can't. We will fall!
Come to the edge.
And they came.
And he pushed them.
And they flew.
—*Guillaume Apollinaire*
French Poet, Philosopher[lxxi]

―――――

Do you remember the television show Dallas? I'm not talking the new one that came out recently, but the original back in the late 1970's. Remember Who shot JR? People were consumed with it. They spent the entire summer talking about who shot a character on a television show.

If we could be obsessed by God the way people were JR, imagine how much better this world would be. However, in this age of faster internet and fast food, we are more enthusiastic with The Walking

Dead than Jesus Christ.

As if televisions and movies don't take our time. We also have children's soccer, football, or dance classes. There's also work and get-togethers with friends and families. All things that take our time from God.

Imagine if your dad had been consumed with raising you to be strong and confident. How different would your life be? We become overwhelmed with things we have to do, leaving God in the if I get time to do pile.

How would your life be different if you put in as much effort with learning about God as you do knowing who won the latest talent contest?

There are 10,080 minutes in a week. How many do you give to God? An hour a week at church, maybe two. Thirty minutes a night for prayer and reading the Bible? If so, that's 330 minutes each week. About three percent (3%) of your time. If you listen to Christian music in the car on the way to work, you can add more, but do you even come close to the ten percent (10%) mark. If so, you might be puffing your chest out, but God doesn't want just ten percent (10%), He wants one hundred percent (100%) of your focus on Him.

We need to have Jesus in the forefront of our minds before anything else.

As I write this, we are heading into a new year. People will post goals like losing weight or getting out of debt. Making time for God might be on their list, but chances are it's near the middle, if even that high.

We become overwhelmed
with things we have to do,
leaving God in the 'if I get time to do' pile.

Yet, God should be at the top of our list. He should become our passion more than work, grandchildren, and writing. (Yes, Kathy, writing.) We settle for idols like big screen televisions and vacations to make us happy only to discover once the new wears off, we want more. We should instead be consumed with the one true joy – God.

He thinks about us from the time He formed us in our mother's womb (Jeremiah 1:5). He even knows the number of hairs on our heads (Matthew 10:30). Yet we give Him fleeting moments in our day.

How close a relationship would you have if you had God tattooed on your palm like He does your name (Isaiah 49:16)? In order to get that deep connection, we have to do the work at it. His work is done. It began when He created us until He reached the cross. It is now up to us to work on this relationship.

How do you get your heart on fire for God: The Bible, fellowship, talking with Him daily, and prayer? There should be no aspect of your life you don't want to discuss with God, from your route to work in the morning to the meal you plan for dinner.

And when you come before Him, spend more time worshipping him, than discussing your problems. Too often we are more interested in making ourselves feel better than in showing God how much we love Him. Don't get me wrong, He wants to hear your problems, but like most of your friends, He'd like you to hear His voice as well. So spend time in peace getting to know Him better. Become intimate with God.

In order to have that closeness of God the Father, we must light the match and become consumed by our faith. If we put our focus on Him, our past will no longer be able to haunt us.

———————

To trust God in the light is nothing,
but trust Him in the dark – that is faith.
—*C.H. Spurgeon*
Baptist Preacher[lxxii]

———————

Let God's Light Shine

Christ cannot light a single spark
in the heart of an individual,
without that little tiny spark being for God.
He gives the light, and has ordained
that every ray of it
is to reflect something for God.
—*G.V. Wigram, Biblical Scholar*[lxxiii]

Too often, we allow our lonely childhood and self-hate to darken our daily walk. Instead, we should show the light of Jesus to others. When you show the Lord's light, it lets others know there is something special about you. That inner glow makes other people want what you have. What does a woman with the light inside her look like? The following are five examples of women that glow with the love of the Lord.

1. The Joyful Woman always wears a smile. You'd be hard pressed to know anything bad is going on in her life because she appears happy wherever she goes. This woman is the person everyone wants to be around. She can find the good in anyone and any situation. To her, laughter is not a sin. It's an escape God gives us from a hectic day. She relies totally on Jesus for every aspect of her life. This woman knows that her savior will get her through rough times so she allows Him total control. And she is willing to give the joy that fills her heart to others so they too may feel the happiness of Jesus Christ.

2. The Grace-Filled woman isn't one to hold a grudge. Her emotions do not rule her. She knows feelings can lie, so she follows the Lord instead. There is nothing anyone can do to her that she cannot endure because she knows God has always

been with her, and during her worst times, He has held her in His arms. She's more than willing to give as much grace as she receives. Forgiveness and love are two of her best attributes. But she also knows the ultimate sign of grace is not her kindness, but in the Cross where her Savior was hung.

3. The Gentle Lady has a quiet tone when dealing with others. There are no harsh words. She uses her voice and a look to exude her emotions, most of which are kind. You might steal from her, but she doesn't berate. Instead, she questions why? Were you hungry and in need of food? Does your child need diapers? You might hurt her emotionally, but she turns to the Lord for her comfort. She is aware that God can heal any broken heart. He is her strength and rock. She gives all that kindness to others in need, helping the downtrodden and those who have lost loved ones. When someone is in need of warmth and love, they seek this woman out.

4. The Humble Woman doesn't take credit for the events in her life. Her demeanor is one of humility. She gives all the accolades to the glory of God. And she means it. Too many people thank the Lord when they win, but then show their non-belief with their lifestyle. We see this in Hollywood and among sports stars all the time. However, this glorious woman of God speaks not only of the virtues of Jesus, but her actions yell louder than her words. She is notorious for giving others credit where it is deserved. She'd rather the spotlight be pointed away. She doesn't need a light to shine on her face because she knows the light of Jesus should shine from within.

5. Finally, there is the Committed Woman. She uses her time to get to know Jesus better. She is aware that her life must depend on Him if she is to be truly happy. She gives no excuses for not reading her Bible because she knows there is none. She is not afraid to pray in public. Her savior is the most important thing in her life, and she will rely on Him for every decision she must make. She is ruthless in her commitment to Jesus Christ. She

shares her faith with others, wanting them to know the love she feels inside.

All the women described above have a special kind of faith. Their staunch belief in God never waivers. Women like these can change the hearts of evil men and change the immorality of a country.

Faithful women can fit into one or more of these categories.

If you look around your church, I'm sure you can spot them. They became close to God by spending time with Him.

Too often we give a little to God and don't feel that all-consuming love we desire. We want to be one of the women above but aren't sure how. The only way to learn is through the Bible and the presence of God in your life.

Yes, time is all it takes.

You have to remember
that far too many people
live in spiritual darkness.
Some sit next to you every day.
Some even in the church pew.
So be the light that leads the way.

Show the light of Jesus Christ everywhere you go whether it is in the workplace or dropping your children off at school in the morning. Live as if your Savior is walking beside you every second of every day. Because He is. The more we remember that the more our relationship will grow. That's one thing all these women above have in common. They know God walks beside them. He is their best friend, so they talk to Him constantly about events in their day.

Too many of us, Christians and non-Christians alike, show only impatience and anger. We think we're entitled to get in first even if we show up late for an appointment. We should be the first served. Our perception of ourselves at times is higher than it should be. Cutting in line, stealing things we want but don't need.

In other areas, that perception is not high enough. For instance, bullying others to make ourselves feel better.

We should let the light of God's love show through us. Jesus said in Matthew 5:14-16, "You are the light of the world. A town built on a hill cannot be hidden. Neither do people light a lamp and put it under a bowl. Instead, they put it on its stand, and it gives light to everyone in the house. In the same way, let your light shine before others, that they may see your good deeds and glorify your Father in heaven."

We are to glow with a heart for Jesus. Transmit that light like a beacon on the stormiest night. Too many people live in darkness, not knowing their worth in the Lord. We must show them the light inside their own hearts as well. But help others without bragging. Announcing to the world what you've done only diminishes the light of God and puts it on you instead. Keep Matthew 6:3 imprinted on your heart, "But when you give to the needy, do not let your left hand know what your right hand is doing."

Let me clarify this. I'm not suggesting you go around and baptize people in the town square. Basically, I want you to show your spiritual fruit without acting like a nut. By going too far, you will only alienate people from Jesus. And unless He's the one telling you to shout His praises in the middle of Publix, then it's just about you getting attention. Instead, be kind to others. Be patient when you're made to wait in line. Smile even when you don't feel like it.

Far too many people live in spiritual darkness. Some sit next to you every day, some even in the church pew. So be the light that leads the way.

In order to do that, we must know our worth in Jesus. You are God's daughter, and your invisible tiara should shine with confidence in knowing how you are loved.

Shine your light
and make a positive impact
on the world;
there is nothing so honorable
as helping improve
the lives of others.
—Roy T. Bennett,
author of The Light in the Heart[lxxiv]

The Longer the Roots, the Sturdier the Tree

Deep roots
are not reached by the frost.
—J.R.R. Tolkien, Author[lxxv]

When someone gets married, they confirm their commitment to one another. These days that commitment doesn't always mean much. Couples aren't as willing to put in the time to make their marriages work.

God sees His followers as His bride. He's made a commitment to us and we should do the same. It's time to confirm your desire to want a deeper relationship to Him.

Like I said earlier, I have a terrible fear of heights. It affects a lot of my life. When I was on vacation with my family as a teen, I wouldn't go up in the Seattle Space Needle while everyone else did. I also hate to fly and driving over bridges is a nightmare. Not good for someone who lives in a city surrounded by water and tall bridges.

I'm even afraid of going on a cruise ship because of how high the boats are. Any time I tell someone this, I get a response like "It's not that bad." Of course not to them. They have no such fear.

The same is true when it comes to surrendering and trusting Jesus. I fully understand that it's easier to say "trust God" when you already do. It's not so easy to step out at the snap of a finger.

When you're going through a difficult time, it's easier to complain and yell than to remain calm and trust in God. At times when we are our most vulnerable and prone to getting upset, the devil is right there to pounce. He'll shout in your ear that God doesn't love us. Funny how Satan has to shout, yet God whispers. Eventually, the evil one will bring up our past and words rush in like, "God doesn't really love you any more than your dad did." We become more miserable than we already do.

At these times, you need to focus on what your head knows to be true to control your emotions. God loves you, that's a given. I've proven it several times with scripture, and God has proven it by the things He's blessed you with, including His body on the cross.

In order to hold fast to God, the Father, you need a good root system in God's word. Even faithful Christians might need to replant the seeds of their faith. Sometimes roots of faith can gray and whither during a drought. We can become complacent in our walk with God.

Like a tree, in order to withstand bad weather, we need a strong root system to withstand a storm. The stronger and deeper our knowledge of the Bible and God, the better able we will be to fight off the storms of life. A newly planted tree is weak. Its roots are not yet established deep in the ground. It takes care, watering, and years for it to become stable in the strongest of storms.

It's the same way with Christians.

We can't just say we think of God as Father. We have to live like we believe it. Time and effort will make us stronger than our doubts.

The more mature you become in your Christian walk, the more likely you can overcome any type of storm that comes your way. By spending time with God, you develop a deeper understanding of how He loves you as His child.

At these times,
you need to focus
on what your head knows
to be true
to control your emotions.
And we know God loves us.

In time, you'll realize His arms are there to hold you when life gets tough. And when a storm hits, you might bend, but you won't break.

Having faith is a wondrous thing. It gives us something to rely on besides ourselves. However, it can also be a scary prospect if we are intent on showing that faith to others. There are always going to be those who put you down. Some will say they don't believe in God because they can't see him. Try not to roll your eyes. They are so lost they couldn't find their elbow with directions. They don't realize that they can't see oxygen but without it, they'd die. And I'm almost certain each time I walk outside I'm not going to float away because gravity will keep me grounded. These are just two things we can't see, yet we all know and trust they are there. We should have the same faith in God.

God, as your loving father, wants you to rely on Him totally. He wants you to have faith that no matter what occurs in your life, He will be there for you.

It doesn't matter what type of father you had growing up, God has been your Heavenly father all along. He is the father you can look up to, hold on to, and trust to be there.

We need to get that ingrained in our minds even if we had earthly fathers who didn't step up. There's nothing that compares to God's love. We are His daughters. He is a king and we are his princesses.

Now say "I am worthy of being God's daughter." Say it again. Still not sure? Post it around your house. If that doesn't make you smile every time you see it, nothing will.

Are you ready to become the daughter of a king? To accept God as your Heavenly Father? If so, sit up straight, place that tiara on the top of your head and announce to the world, "God is my true Father, and I am His princess."

Pull your hair up into a ponytail and allow your ponytail to swing in the wind. If your hair's not long enough, just sway your head back and forth. Such a freeing feeling to know He is out there, and we can depend on Him totally.

Once we recognize our need for Jesus,
then the building of our faith begins.
It is a daily, moment-by-moment life
of absolute dependence upon Him
for everything.
—*Catherine Marshall,*
Author of the Christy Book Series[lxxvi]

Bible Verse

We must seek God in order to have a personal relationship with Him. He's never left us, we were the ones who stepped back. The following tells of David's longing to have God in His life. We have that yearning as well.

Psalm 63:1-8

You, God, are my God,
earnestly I seek you;
I thirst for you,
my whole being longs for you,
in a dry and parched land
where there is no water.
I have seen you in the sanctuary
and beheld your power and your glory.
Because your love is better than life,
my lips will glorify you.
I will praise you as long as I live,
and in your name I will lift up my hands.
I will be fully satisfied as with the richest of foods;
with singing lips my mouth will praise you.
On my bed I remember you;
I think of you through the watches of the night.
Because you are my help,
I sing in the shadow of your wings.
I cling to you;
your right hand upholds me.

We see in these verses how David has a thirst for God. David used such good words to describe his desire. Words like "parched" told of the dryness in his life. He goes on to say he will not only glorify God with praise, but with song as well. David advices us to "cling" to God when times get hard. The more we rely on Him, the sooner our relationship will become that of daughter and father.

Closing Prayer

Father,

You are wonderful. Thank You for all the great verses in the Bible that show me that I am indeed Your child. Thank You for giving me Jesus as a way to You, so I will be forgiven and can spend eternity at Your table. Please hold me when times get rough and remind me I am a princess to a wonderful King. Show me ways I can spend more time with you to deepen our relationship. Thank you for being my father. I love You, Lord.

In Jesus name,

Amen

To Dig Deeper:

A. Here are some questions to help you dig a bit deeper into your relationship with God.

1. In the section titled "Let God's Light Shine;" we discussed women consumed with God who show His light to others. Which Godly woman would you like to be? What one thing can you do to begin to accomplish that goal?

2. How often do you spend on the computer or watching television each day? How often do you spend with God? Matthew 6:21 tells us that "…where your treasure is, there your heart will be also." This goes for your time as well. Knowing this, what are you willing to give up for more time with God?

3. Have you ever tried to pull a weed from the ground, but it didn't want to come no matter how hard you tugged? That's the way it can be with your faith in God. The more time spent with Him, the less likely to be pulled away in times of strife. In

what ways will you work to grow a stronger root system in your relationship with God?

4. Have you ever been really thirsty? So thirsty you were parched as described in Psalm 63 above? How does that dryness compare with your relationship with God? Are you thirsty, somewhat thirsty, really thirsty, or parched?

5. How has your view on God the Father changed since beginning this book? Stronger, weaker, no change? Do you feel you can see Him in a different light than your earthly father?

6. How will you spend your time getting to know God better? What do you expect from this newfound relationship with God the Father?

Read the following Bible verses. How does each verse show God's love for you?

1. John 1:4-5: "In him was life, and that life was the light of all mankind. The light shines in the darkness, and the darkness has not overcome it."

a. Have you ever had one of those days where you felt like you looked good to the point you almost glowed? Maybe people walked by smiling and saying hello? It's a great feeling. I think that's when our light shines. Remember back to that day. What was different than any other day?

b. Flip off the light or go to a dark room. Now turn on a flashlight or even your cell phone. See how it stands out in the dark? We are to shine like that in the dark world. What do you think you can do to shine Jesus' light for others?

2. Ephesians 2:8-10: "For it is by grace you have been saved, through faith—and this is not from yourselves, it is the gift of God— not by works, so that no one can boast. For we are God's

handiwork, created in Christ Jesus to do good works, which God prepared in advance for us to do."

a. Other than God's gifts, what has been the best present you've ever received? (I'm talking Christmas or birthday gifts – those type of presents.) Do you still have it? If not, what did you do with it?

b. Why do you feel God has put you here on Earth? Usually it's got to do with a passion you feel inside. What's your passion, and how can you use it for God's benefit?

3. John 15:1-8: "I am the true vine, and my Father is the gardener. He cuts off every branch in me that bears no fruit, while every branch that does bear fruit he prunes so that it will be even more fruitful. You are already clean because of the word I have spoken to you. Remain in me, as I also remain in you. No branch can bear fruit by itself; it must remain in the vine. Neither can you bear fruit unless you remain in me. "I am the vine; you are the branches. If you remain in me and I in you, you will bear much fruit; apart from me you can do nothing. If you do not remain in me, you are like a branch that is thrown away and withers; such branches are picked up, thrown into the fire and burned. If you remain in me and my words remain in you, ask whatever you wish, and it will be done for you. This is to my Father's glory, that you bear much fruit, showing yourselves to be my disciples."

a. God is the gardener, chopping away on us to get rid of things that bear no fruit, like pride and being judgmental (two of my issues). What does He need to trim away from you? What type of fruit would you like to grow in order to help others get to know God?

b. Picture all the branches you could have if you allowed God to work in you. How big would your tree be? What type of fruit would you like your largest branches to hold?

4. Proverbs 3:5-6: "Trust in the Lord with all your heart and lean not on your own understanding; in all your ways submit to him, and he will make your paths straight."

a. Sometimes we make up our minds about something a bit faster than we should, not waiting and thinking things through. What has been the biggest mistake you've ever made because you didn't take a step back and do more research?

b. Submission is a hard one for Americans, especially women. We've had too many men in our lives think we should follow their lead, even when it wasn't good for us. How do you see submission to God? Is it in a good light or bad? Does it make you nervous or secure?

5. Job 11:13-15: "Surrender your heart to God, turn to him in prayer, and give up your sins—even those you do in secret. Then you won't be ashamed; you will be confident and fearless."

a. Some alcoholics hide their alcohol in the hopes no one finds out they're still drinking. Overeaters might hide candy. Do you have something you hide that you don't want anyone to know about? One of the best ways to get over it is to share that secret with another. If you don't feel comfortable telling someone else, tell God. Let Him help you to come clean.

b. I would love to be fearless – have no fear of heights, not worry when that strange looking guy is heading my way. What is your fear? How can you use God in order to get over that fear?

CONCLUSION

Well, this is the end. The final pages. The finale.

My hope is that this book helped you to realize God is nothing like your abusive or neglectful father.

Sometimes I'm not sure why God has me write some of the things He does. It could be for your benefit, but in the end, I really think it's for mine. He's sneaky that way. He's like a father who makes yummy noises to convince you those Brussel sprouts taste good when they really don't. No offense to the Brussels sprout fans.

What an amazing Father we have.

I hope you walk away from this book feeling a deeper relationship with God and are able to at least begin to look upon Him as your Father. Remember how much He loves you. And no matter what anyone says, you are a princess. You are the one and only true child of a king. I hope you now have the faith and courage to accept his hand as you continue your journey with Him.

And thank you for being my sister in Christ. Our family can never get too big.

God bless you all.
Kathryn J. Bain

RESOURCES

i 66 Best International Women's Day Quotes, March 8, 2015, http://www.quotesigma.com/67-best-international-womens-day-quotes/

ii Grace quotes, A Place of Quiet Rest, Moody, 2000, p 43, Nancy Leigh DeMoss, Tyndale House Publishing, http://gracequotes.org/quote/the-christian-life-is-not-about-all-the-things-we/; accessed December 2, 2016

iii Saint Augustine. BrainyQuote.com, Xplore Inc, 2017. https://www.brainyquote.com/quotes/quotes/s/saintaugus105351.html, accessed February 14, 2017

iv http://www.goodreads.com/quotes/643934-the-sin-underneath-all-our-sins-is-to-trust-the; accessed December 3, 2016

v "God as Father," by John Servidio, https://lifehopeandtruth.com/god/who-is-god/god-as-a-father/

vi "Jesus is Lord, God's Love Spritual Exercises," http://www.aggiecatholic.org/documents/2015/10/Prayer%20Exercises%20-%20Gods%20Love%20revised.pdf

vii 10 reasons Fathers are so Important to their daughters, www.holidappy.com/holidays/10-reasons-Fathers-are-so-Important-to-their-Daughters

viii "Suicide Rate Triples Among Girls," by Kimberly Leonard, http://www.usnews.com/news/articles/2016-04-22/cdc-suicide-deaths-on-the-rise-among-teen-girls-and-middle-aged-men.

ix Old Quotes, http://www.oldquotes.com/single.php?u=life-is-hard-unfair-it-is-cruel-heartless-painful-trying-disappointing-unapologetic-frequently-downright-awful-but-thats-not-important-whats-important-is-that-through-it-all-you-learn-how-much-you-need-your-heavenly-father-how-much-your-friends-need-you-richelle-e-goodrich&id=156723; accessed December 15, 2016

[x] "The 'Confessio' of Saint Patrick," https://www.ccel.org/ccel/patrick/confession.txt

[xi] Jason Kirk Bartley, "Father of Light," http://www.a-spiritual-journey-of-healing.com/god-the-father-poems.html'

[xii] "The Nicene Creed," http://anglicansonline.org/basics/nicene.html

[xiii] http://www.goodreads.com/quotes/1027273-the-more-i-contemplate-god-the-more-god-looks-on; accessed December 27, 2016

[xiv] http://www.picturequotes.com/if-i-could-change-one-thing-about-myself-it-would-be-the-voices-in-my-head-they-dont-like-me-quote-7292; accessed December 27, 2016

[xv] The Fatherless Daughter Project, http://fatherlessdaughterproject.com/about-you/

[xvi] "Seeing Yourself and Others as Beautiful," by Grace Houle, http://www.pouredouthislove.com/

[xvii] http://a-thousand-words.tumblr.com/post/95395613528/time-heals-all-wounds-and-if-it-doesnt-you-name

[xviii] Helen Keller. BrainyQuote.com, Xplore Inc, 2017. https://www.brainyquote.com/quotes/quotes/h/helenkelle152190.html, accessed February 14, 2017

[xix] Forty Thousand Quotations: Prose and Poetical, comp. by Charles Noel Douglas. New York: Halcyon House, 1917; Bartleby.com, 2012, "Abraham Lincoln." www.bartleby.com/348. accessed February 14, 2017.

[xx] Jon Bloom, "Your Emotions Are a Gauge, Not a Guide,"August 3, 2012, http://www.desiringgod.org/articles/your-emotions-are-a-gauge-not-a-guide

[xxi] "Seeing Yourself As God Sees You," by Marcia Greenwood, https://www.tgm.org/SeeingYourselfAsGodSeesYou.html

[xxii] Positive Quotes "Love of Self," http://systemagicmotives.com/Quotations/Love%20of%20Self%20Quotes.htm; accessed February 14, 2017

[xxiii] Leigh McLeroy, "Does God Care When I Hurt?" Explore God, http://www.exploregod.com/does-god-care-when-i-hurt.

xxiv Child Sexual Abuse Statistics, https://victimsofcrime.org/media/reporting-on-child-sexual-abuse/child-sexual-abuse-statistics

xxv "Cancer in Children and Adolescents," National Cancer Institute, https://www.cancer.gov/types/childhood-cancers/child-adolescent-cancers-fact-sheet#q1

xxvi http://www.goodreads.com/quotes/462510-riches-take-wings-comforts-vanish-hope-withers-away-but-love-stays; accessed January 20, 2017

xxvii Mortimer Adler. BrainyQuote.com, Xplore Inc, 2017. https://www.brainyquote.com/quotes/quotes/m/mortimerad204041.html, accessed February 14, 2017.

xxviii Dodinsky quotes, http://izquotes.com/quote/294790, accessed February 14, 2017

xxix Eleanor Roosevelt. BrainyQuote.com, Xplore Inc, 2017. https://www.brainyquote.com/quotes/quotes/e/eleanorroo121157.html, accessed February 14, 2017

xxx Work: A Story of Experience, by Louisa May Alcott, pg. 148, pub. 1904

xxxi http://www.goodreads.com/quotes/tag/resting-in-god, Sue Detweiler, 9 Traits of a Life-Giving Mom: Replacing My Worst with God's Best, accessed January 20, 2017

xxxii Robert Menzies. BrainyQuote.com, Xplore Inc, 2017. https://www.brainyquote.com/quotes/quotes/r/robertmenz117536.html, accessed February 14, 2017

xxxiii "Let it Go!" by Judith Sills, Ph.D., November 4, 2014, https://www.psychologytoday.com/articles/201411/let-it-go

xxxiv 120 Quotes to Inspire Letting Go of Attachments (Tips), http://sepitajima.com/120-quotes-on-letting-go-of-attachments-tips/, accessed February 14, 2017

xxxv http://www.goodreads.com/quotes/6754512-don-t-be-afraid-to-stand-tall-in-your-truth-boldly, accessed February 14, 2017

xxxvi "Father Absence, Father Deficit, Father Hunger," by Edward Kruk, Ph.D, May 23, 2012, https://www.psychologytoday.com/blog/co-parenting-after-divorce/201205/father-absence-father-deficit-father-hunger

xxxvii "Two Words to Stop Self-Condemnation," Christine Hoover, March 4, 2015, http://www.desiringgod.org/articles/two-words-to-stop-self-condemnation

xxxviii "Trauma is Personal," by Danielle Bernock, July 6, 2016, http://www.

daniellebernock.com/traumaispersonal/

[xxxix] "The Second Assault," by Olga Khazan, The Atlantic, December 15, 2015, http://www.theatlantic.com/health/archive/2015/12/sexual-abuse-victims-obesity/420186/

[xl] Elbert Hubbard. BrainyQuote.com, Xplore Inc, 2017. https://www.brainyquote.com/quotes/quotes/e/elberthubb384301.html, accessed February 14, 2017.

[xli] "Ask Deepak: How to Stop Feeling Self-Pity," by Deepak Chopra, http://www.oprah.com/spirit/how-to-stop-feeling-self-pity-ask-deepak

[xlii] "How Volunteering Can Lesson Depression and Extend Your Life," by Sara Konrath, Ph.D., August 22, 2013, http://www.everydayhealth.com/depression/how-volunteering-can-lessen-depression-and-extend-your-life.aspx

[xliii] "The Mental Health Benefits of Exercise," Helpguide.org, http://www.helpguide.org/articles/exercise-fitness/emotional-benefits-of-exercise.htm

[xliv] Maya Angelou. BrainyQuote.com, Xplore Inc, 2017. https://www.brainyquote.com/quotes/quotes/m/mayaangelo110545.html, accessed February 16, 2017

[xlv] http://www.goodreads.com/quotes/322935-we-are-all-unkind-from-time-to-time-we-all; accessed February 2, 2017

[xlvi] "5 Steps to Forgiving Yourself," by Sarah Markley, December 2, 2012, http://www.incourage.me/2012/12/5-steps-to-forgiving-yourself.html

[xlvii] https://twitter.com/stevenfurtick/status/67981913746444288?lang=en; accessed February 9, 2017

[xlviii] "Warning: Stop Comparing Yourself to Others," by Tania Kotsos, http://www.mind-your-reality.com/comparing_yourself_to_others.html

[xlix] Rick Warren sermon, 10/21/13, http://www.fbc-moline.org/sermons/Do_Something_Beautiful_for_God.pdf

[l] Dorothy Corkille Briggs. BrainyQuote.com, Xplore Inc, 2017. https://www.brainyquote.com/quotes/quotes/d/dorothycor403925.html, accessed February 14, 2017

[li] Rabindranath Tagore. BrainyQuote.com, Xplore Inc, 2017. https://www.brainyquote.com/quotes/quotes/r/rabindrana121379.html, accessed February 16, 2017.

[lii] "The Meaning of REAL Surrender to God," David A. DePra, http://www.

goodnewsarticles.com/Apr07-2.htm

liii http://www.sermonindex.net/modules/articles/index.php?view=article&aid=33017

liv "The Love of God," Dieter F. Uchtdorf, https://www.lds.org/general-conference/2009/10/the-love-of-god?lang=eng

lv Reverend David DePra, "The Good News" "The Meaning of REAL Surrender to God," David A. DePra, http://www.goodnewsarticles.com/Apr07-2.htm

lvi The Ragamuffin Gospel: Good News for the Bedraggled, Beat Up, and Burnt Out, Brennan Manning, pub. Multnomah, page 90.

lvii Humbly Submitting to Change, by E'yen Gardner, Print World Publishing, October 21, 2010

lviii Faith Deployed Again: More Daily Encouragement for Military Wives, by Jocelyn Green, Moody Publishers, July 1, 2011

lix Confucius. BrainyQuote.com, Xplore Inc, 2017. https://www.brainyquote.com/quotes/quotes/c/confucius101164.html, accessed February 15, 2017

lx "Billy Graham: Fruit Grows in Valleys," Henriet Schapelhouman, August 13, 2010, http://www.henrietsblog.com/2010/08/billy-graham-fruit-grows-in-valleys.html#.V_SW1PkrLX4.

lxi Anne F. Beiler. BrainyQuote.com, Xplore Inc, 2017. https://www.brainyquote.com/quotes/quotes/a/annefbeil582001.html, accessed February 15, 2017

lxii http://www.quotegarden.com/crying.html, accessed February 12, 2017

lxiii "The Muddled Tracks of All Those Tears," by Benedict Carey, February 2, 2009, http://www.nytimes.com/2009/02/03/health/03mind.html?_r=1&ref=science

lxiv https://en.wikiquote.org/wiki/John_Vance_Cheney, accessed February 15, 2017

lxv http://www.goodreads.com/quotes/835145-t-hou-canst-not-think-worse-of-me-than-i-do, accessed February 15, 2017

lxvi One Thousand Gifts: A Dare to Live Fully Right Where You Are, By Ann Voskamp, pub. Zondervan, January 4, 2011

lxvii Kilimanjaro and Beyond: A Life-Changing Journey, by Barry Finlay, pub. Dog Ear

Publishing, June 30, 2011

[lxviii] Amelia Barr. BrainyQuote.com, Xplore Inc, 2017. https://www.brainyquote.com/quotes/quotes/a/ameliabarr202842.html, accessed February 16, 2017

[lxix] https://www.christianquotes.info/top-quotes/16-powerful-quotes-remember-youre-afraid/#axzz4YlDVKsaw, accessed February 2, 2017

[lxx] http://www.whatchristianswanttoknow.com/21-awesome-christian-quotes-about-women/; accessed February 2, 2017

[lxxi] http://www.goodreads.com/quotes/17760-come-to-the-edge-he-said-we-can-t-we-re-afraid; accessed February 3, 2017

[lxxii] https://www.dailyinspirationalquotes.in/2016/03/trust-god-light-nothing-trust-dark-faith-c-h-spurgeon/; accessed February 3, 2017

[lxxiii] The Writings of George Vicesimus Wigram: Memorials Volume Two, Ecclesiastical, Critical, Letters, Gleanings, Short Papers, and Other Writings, by George Vicesimus Wigram

[lxxiv] http://www.briefquotes.com/tag/shine-your-light/, #17, accessed February 2, 2017

[lxxv] J. R. R. Tolkien. BrainyQuote.com, Xplore Inc, 2017.

https://www.brainyquote.com/quotes/quotes/j/jrrtolk629293.html, accessed February 15, 2017

[lxxvi] A Woman's Garden of Faith, by Freeman-Smith, Pub. Freeman Smith, February 28, 2013

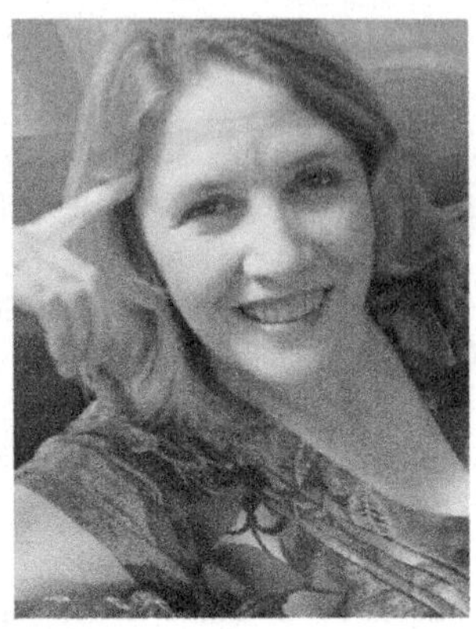

ABOUT KATHRYN J. BAIN

Award-winning fiction author Kathryn J. Bain takes her first step into the realm of nonfiction with her latest book *Holding the Hand of a King.*

Not only is she a co-leader of LOL, (Ladies of the Lord), the Tuesday night Bible study group in her church, she is also a past President of Florida Sisters in Crime and Public Relations Director for Ancient City Romance Authors. She also has a small Facebook Group for Christian writers called Writers for Jesus.

Ms. Bain has over ten fiction books available, some of which have garnered awards including First Place for Short Suspense in the IDA (Independent Digital Awards) and a First Place Royal Palm Literary Award for Inspirational Fiction.

Kathryn has also been a paralegal for over twenty years and works for an attorney who specializes in elder law.

Made in the USA
Monee, IL
07 July 2026